great kitchens
collection

Great American Kitchens Collection
Editor: Amy Tincher-Durik
Contributing Editor: Olivia Bell Buehl
Senior Associate Design Director: Chad Jewell
Contributing Graphic Designer: Joseph Kantorski
Copy Chief: Terri Fredrickson
Account Manager: Donna Olin
Publishing Operations Manager: Karen Schirm
Edit and Design Production Coordinator: Mary Lee Gavin
Book Production Managers: Pam Kvitne, Marjorie J. Schenkelberg, Rick von Holdt, Mark Weaver
Contributing Proofreader: Dan Degen
Indexer: Beverly Nightenshelser
Editorial Assistant: Kaye Chabot
Cover Photograph: Michael Hewes/www.michaelhewes.com

Meredith® Books
Editor in Chief: Linda Raglan Cunningham
Design Director: Matt Strelecki
Managing Editor: Gregory H. Kayko
Executive Editor: Denise L. Caringer

Publisher: James D. Blume
Executive Director, Marketing: Jeffrey Myers
Executive Director, New Business Development: Todd M. Davis
Executive Director, Sales: Ken Zagor
Director, Operations: George A. Susral
Director, Production: Douglas M. Johnston
Business Director: Jim Leonard

Vice President and General Manager: Douglas J. Guendel

Meredith Publishing Group
President, Publishing Group: Stephen M. Lacy
Vice President-Publishing Director: Bob Mate

Meredith Corporation
Chairman and Chief Executive Officer: William T. Kerr

In Memoriam: E. T. Meredith III (1933-2003)

All of us at Meredith® Books are dedicated to providing you with information and ideas to enhance your home. We welcome your comments and suggestions. Write to us at: Meredith Books, Home Decorating and Design Editorial Department, 1716 Locust St., Des Moines, IA 50309-3023.

If you would like to purchase any of our home decorating and design, cooking, crafts, gardening, or home improvement books, check wherever quality books are sold. Or visit us at: meredithbooks.com

great american
kitchens
collection

MEREDITH® BOOKS
DES MOINES, IOWA

great american
kitchens
collection

66

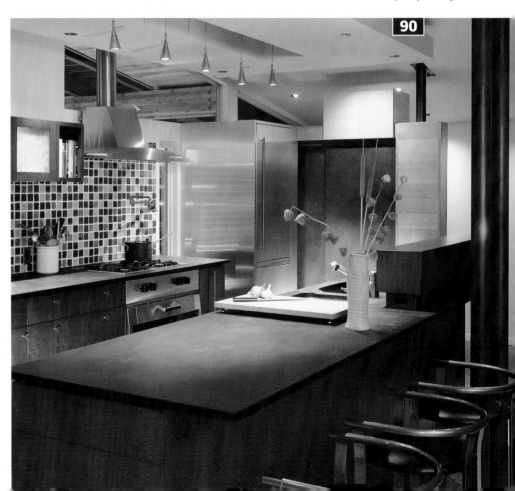

90

On the cover: Molding atop the cabinets defines the ceiling line, while quartersawn cherry forms a uniform vertical grain pattern throughout the space. The kitchen, which features the Sub-Zero Model 632/S refrigerator-freezer, was designed by Catherine Scott of Catherine B. Scott Residential Design. Photography by Michael Hewes/www.michaelhewes.com

great american
kitchens
collection

144

On page 1: A mix of stainless steel and white—on the walls and streamlined cabinets—keeps this kitchen light and bright. Designed by Arlene Pilson, of Arlene Pilson Interior Design. Photography by George Ross. See page 84 for more on this kitchen.

On page 3: Distressed paint finishes, furniture details, and colorful tiles give this kitchen old-world charm. Designed by Charles Buller. Photography by Jon Jensen. See page 198 for more on this kitchen.

118

great american
kitchens
collection

dream big

From the time the first cave dwellers eagerly huddled over open fires, mealtimes have been the day's highlights. They were chances to share food and friendship—and bond with family and community.

Happily, we don't have to crouch in caves for our meals anymore. But the significance of the kitchen to families everywhere is even more important today. Quite simply, it's where we love to gather—and it's often the most popular room in the house. We yearn to sample what's cookin' ... to share special times with friends and family ... to be surrounded by our beloved objects ... and to be comforted by the personal style our particular kitchen reflects.

That's where the *Great American Kitchens Collection* comes in. This gorgeous book is packed with all the dream kitchens—each of which was a winner in the Sub-Zero Freezer Company/Wolf kitchen design contest—you need to engage and inspire you. Love the sleek sophistication of contemporary style? Admire the look of updated country, with distressed finishes and unexpected colors? Maybe the genteel simplicity of old-world decorating soothes you with its echoes of centuries past. Or perhaps your love of the outdoors and contrasting textures translates to a rugged style. Regardless of the style that reflects your personality, you are sure to find myriad ideas throughout this book: Each section includes kitchens of a particular style, from sleek and streamlined contemporary to the spicy colors and exotic materials of kitchens with ethnic flair.

Whether you live in a New York City condo, a Colorado lodge, or a Florida '50s ranch, the design professionals featured throughout this book can help you translate the looks you love into ideas for your ideal kitchen. (We even give you their names and contact information starting on page 281.)

To jump-start your next kitchen adventure, check out the latest innovations in kitchen appliances on page 9, turn to page 14 to learn how homeowners from across the country are putting their personal stamp on their kitchens—from displaying collections to choosing color schemes that evoke a wide array of moods—and see page 18 to discover more about what's hot now in kitchen design. And, when you are ready to start the journey, look to the kitchen planning kit, beginning on page 277; it's just what you need to begin to create the kitchen you've always wanted.

So peruse these dramatic spaces. See what strikes your fancy. Discover a look that says "you." Start planning. Dream big. And, most of all, enjoy the exciting inspiration waiting for you in the following pages.

Right: Cooking is more fun when you know your dish will come out perfectly, as it will with the right cooking equipment. The Wolf 60-inch-wide gas range and hood complement any style kitchen. **Below:** A single knob controls eight different cook modes in the Wolf dual-fuel range. The digital readout shows the actual oven temperature.

h●t stuff

■ As the true "living" room, the kitchen merits special attention when it comes to selecting appliances, cabinets, and accessories. Sub-Zero and Wolf appliances come in a stunning variety that allows smart homeowners—in concert with design professionals—to select appliances that not only boast a host of innovative features, but also best suit the individual needs of their users. The quality cooking and refrigeration appliances from Sub-Zero and Wolf that appear on the following pages are made for people who are passionate about both food and superb design.

welcome

For nearly 60 years, Sub-Zero has pioneered in technical innovations as well as design excellence. Unique to Sub-Zero, and indicative of the company's trendsetting engineering, its dual-refrigeration system relies on two separate, self-contained cooling systems to keep fresh food fresher and preserve frozen food longer.

We also have a comprehensive line of built-ins developed in response to your needs. With the state-of-the-art 400 Series, Sub-Zero has made wine storage both beautiful and functional. The design-flexible 600 Series can address virtually any kitchen design challenge. With the integrated 700 Series, refrigeration can move beyond the confines of the kitchen and be concealed in cabinetry throughout the home.

With this heritage, it's no wonder that not long ago when Sub-Zero was seeking a corporate companion in the cooking arena, it acquired Wolf Appliance Company. For 70 plus years, the name Wolf has been synonymous with top-of-the-line professional cooking equipment.

Now, as part of Sub-Zero, the Wolf line has been expanded for the serious home cook. Every Wolf product is designed from the ground up to give the user ultimate control and cooking confidence. Testing ensures that products not only meet, but exceed, industry standards. Moreover, each is backed by one of the best warranties in the business.

I am very proud to be the third generation of family owners and managers of Sub-Zero. Now Wolf is part of the same proud family. We call our two brands kitchen soul mates because they carry on the tradition of innovation started by my grandfather, Westye Bakke, in 1945, and continued by my father, Bud.

James J. Bakke
PRESIDENT AND CEO
SUB-ZERO FREEZER COMPANY
WOLF APPLIANCE COMPANY

hot stuff

1 The best of two cooking worlds: Together, the Wolf dual-convection gas cooktop and electric oven (Model DF484C6 is shown here) provide ultimate control and versatility.

2 The Wolf electric cooktop ensures one-touch control and ultimate flexibility. The triple 12-inch element can deliver a powerful 2,700 watts of energy. The cooktop is available in 15-, 30-, and 36-inch widths.

3 At the other extreme, in addition to the simmer setting, the melt function offers extremely low temperature control. Precise adjustment is simple; settings can be locked for child safety.

4 The ceramic bake stone in all Wolf dual-fuel ranges and wall ovens guarantees crisp-crust pizzas and superb bread. The kit also comes with its own rack and an easy-to-plug-in electric element.

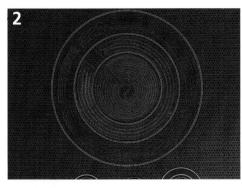

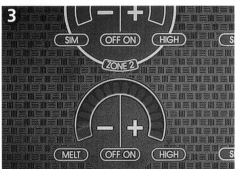

"We call
our brands
kitchen
soul
mates."
—James J. Bakke

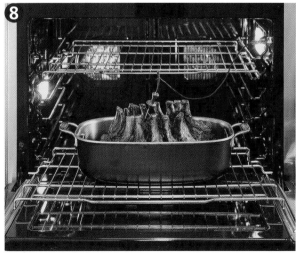

5 The glass-enclosed control panel for the Wolf dual-fuel range is revealed with the push of a finger. It controls the oven's time functions and special features.

6 Patented dual-stacked sealed burners are a feature on all Wolf gas cooktops and dual-fuel ranges. They can adjust from a tiny flame to searing heat.

7 Six different Wolf 15-inch modules allow ultimate cooking personalization. Shown, from left: fryer, grill, and two-burner gas units. Also available: a two-element electric cooktop, a multifunctional high-output unit, and a steamer.

8 The Wolf exclusive dual-convection system delivers even temperature and airflow throughout the oven. Two fans couple with four heating elements to offer flexibility without complex controls. Other pluses are the blue porcelain interior and an exclusive bottom shelf that pulls out on grooves in the open door.

hot stuff

9 This Wolf 30-inch-wide, four-burner gas cooktop provides maximum firepower. All the dual-stacked sealed burners can simmer. Two burners can heat to 12,000 BTUs; the other two can reach 9,200 BTUs. Model CT30G, shown below, is available in classic or platinum stainless steel.

10 A glass oven-control panel plays hide-and-seek on all Wolf wall ovens. When not in use, the panel quietly rotates out of sight for a sleek appearance.

11 Wolf warming drawers offer improved airflow and hidden electronic controls. Added features include interchangeable stainless-steel fronts, the option to attach a cabinet front, and an optional container system for any food. Model WD36/S is shown here.

12 Sub-Zero offers the most complete inventory of built-in refrigeration units on the market. A handsome carbon stainless-steel finish (Model 650/B is shown here) is available on all units. You can also choose from classic or platinum stainless steel.

14 Sub-Zero takes wine storage to a new level with this freestanding addition to the line. Model 424FS accommodates 46 bottles; larger models store 78, 132, and 147 bottles in separately controlled compartments that maintain ideal temperatures for reds and whites.

15 Wolf wall ovens come in both 30- and 36-inch widths; three different stainless-steel finishes; and can be either framed or unframed. Model S030U/B is shown with a Wolf convection microwave.

16 The 36-inch-wide Model S036U/P in platinum stainless steel can be installed below counter or higher on the wall. When not in use, the retractable display panel has a flush appearance.

13 Another addition to the Sub-Zero lineup is this unique model with a glass refrigerator door. Triple-pane UV-treated glass ensures energy efficiency. Like all Sub-Zero combo refrigerator-freezers, it has a dual compressor system. The 30-inch-wide Model 611G/S is shown above. The glass door is also offered in a 36-inch-wide over-and-under model.

trend watch

Today's winning kitchens display a wealth of creative diversity that reflects the personality of the owners.

getting
personal

■ Kitchens that are handsome, functional, and easy to maintain are now a given, but the ante has been upped: A kitchen now must also reflect the owners' personalities and interests. "Today's kitchen designs are idiosyncratic and include offbeat elements," says interior designer Jamie Drake, ASID, of Drake Design Associates in New York City. "By definition, personality-plus details such as a piece of retro signage or stools wearing cowboy boots are not for everyone, but that's exactly the point," Drake adds.

The Importance of Individuality

Today's great American kitchens have personalities all their own. The most personal kitchens actually tell the homeowners' story, says B. Leslie Hart, a journalist and a member of the National Kitchen & Bath Association's Hall of Fame. "These kitchens say, 'This is who I am and what I've accomplished.'" Joan Kohn, a Chicago-based design expert, host of the HGTV series "Kitchen Design" and "Bed and Bath Design," and author of *Your Kitchen*, agrees that many of the best designs are a "celebration of self. It's as if owners have finally realized that they can do what they want." The result: "A kitchen where you just know by looking at it that they had a great time designing it. And it's not only full of personality, it's also a nice place to work in."

This growing sense of individuality means that "some accepted design rules are no longer considered law," points out designer Mick De Giulio, of de Giulio Kitchen Design, Inc., in Wilmette, Illinois. Instead, rules are questioned and certain elements, such as upper cabinets, may be omitted.

Still, other kitchens gain their individuality from a mixed vocabulary of elements, including features as diverse as an industrial rinser and a salvaged screen door. Increasingly, kitchens include display space for found objects, collectibles, or even fine art.

In some instances, the kitchen is so personalized that it's evident that "the owners have every intention of staying in the house and are not necessarily concerned with resale value," points out Hart. "It's as if people are saying, 'We're more confident of our tastes and this is the kitchen we've always wanted.'"

Celebrating Color

Of course, color is one of the simplest and most direct ways to bring personality into a kitchen. Generally, people are more fearless and willing to express their personality with color, from the subtlest pastel ceiling to crayon-bright blues on banquette upholstery, Drake points out. Depending on the owner's taste and comfort level, color might extend to cabinets enlivened with bold aniline stains. Or it could appear as a deep-toned floor, a colorful countertop material, or a single element, such as a unique tile mural that becomes a focal point.

Look Down, Look Up

Today, creatively planned kitchens treat not just the cabinets and countertops as part of the design, but the floor and ceiling as well. "There's more attention being paid to the entire envelope of space," says De Giulio. Floor details, such as dance steps laid into terrazzo, stripes or insets of unusual tile, and wood laid in a herringbone pattern, further define the space. Many winning kitchens also include interesting ceiling details, such as arches, beams, and vaulted, coffered, and barreled styles, as well as curved recesses that

---

1. Salvaged kitsch puts a dash of flamboyant fun into the beach-house kitchen created by the design team of Pietro Giorgi, Sr., Ellen Cheever, and Gregory Gorrell. See page 138 for this kitchen. 2. This kitchen, designed by Yves Claude, is filled with stainless steel and marble—and resides in an antiques-filled home. For more, see page 31. 3. Treading lightly—and brightly—a series of dance steps highlights the terrazzo floor in the kitchen of architect Clint Pehrson. See page 98 for this kitchen. 4. Designers Earl A. Miller, CKD, and Jody Theobald created an Asian-themed kitchen filled with natural materials—including wood, glass, and stone—that reflects a Japanese influence throughout the home. For more, see page 256.

1

2

3

4

5

6

LEFT: PHOTOGRAPHY: © ROBERT RECK; STYLING: NINA WILLIAMS; RIGHT: PHOTOGRAPHY: SARGENT ARCHITECTURAL PHOTOGRAPHY; STYLING: GINA COOKE-SCOTT

7

8

LEFT: PHOTOGRAPHY: FRAN BRENNAN; STYLING: JOETTA MOULDEN; WWW.SHELTERSTYLE.COM; RIGHT: PHOTOGRAPHY: © PETER RYMWID

create "distinctive, not so right-out-of-the-box spaces," De Giulio adds.

Clean-Lined Classics

Traditional styles remain the choice of many, but traditionally inspired kitchens are becoming streamlined and simplified. "The ornamentation of the last few years—the grapes and filigree elements—is gone and now there's greater emphasis on the integrity of the materials and how they are used," says architect Jeffrey Demure, AIA, of Bloodgood, Sharp, Buster Architects & Planners in El Dorado Hills, California. "We've always seen that emphasis in contemporary designs, but now even the more traditional spaces are moving into exploring the essence of form and material."

This attention to materials translates into less visual clutter, including, for example, the growing use of flat-paneled cabinet doors with a gorgeous finish that shows off the wood grain. Designers are relying on familiar materials, such as glass, used creatively. "We see it in all forms and many applications—glass tile and sheets of glass, used in range hoods and tabletops," notes kitchen designer Fu-Tung Cheng, of Cheng Design in Berkeley, California.

On the contemporary side of the design ledger, the use of both lush natural materials and curved shapes dispels the hard-edged look once associated with modern design. Unusual woods such as anigre and bubinga are also increasingly in evidence. Thus, contemporary design too has become more timeless, says kitchen designer Tom Kelly, of NorthShore Kitchens Plus, Inc., in Marblehead, Massachusetts.

Get Comfortable

There's more interest in integrating what really goes on in the kitchen into the design, says Demure. That translates into dedicated areas for cooking, doing homework, surfing the Internet, or visiting with friends. Families

5. Upholstered chairs make a comfortable sitting area in a Colorado kitchen designed by Ricki Brown. See page 238 for this kitchen. **6.** Full-length windows in the eating area of a kitchen designed by Trish Meyer and decorated by Richard Hoffman maximize a dramatic ocean view. For more, see page 86. **7.** Architect Leonard G. Lane, Jr., tucked a raised table at one end of an island. This kitchen is featured on page 44. **8.** Designer Diane Boyer used limestone and wrought iron for a Mediterranean-style hearth. See page 220 for this kitchen.

increasingly watch television in the kitchen, so TV units are now bigger and bolder. In many cases, they're no longer hidden away behind cabinet doors, but integrated into the kitchen design.

With the kitchen encroaching upon the living room as the center of family life and the place to entertain friends, comfortable seating is a must. More upholstered chairs, banquettes, and even sofas are turning up in the kitchen. "A banquette is far cozier and more comfortable than having to line up on bar stools," says Hart. And when stools are used, those that are ergonomically designed for comfort are favored.

It's All About the View

Today's winning kitchens take full advantage of indoor/outdoor relationships and welcome natural light in all its glory. When there's a view of woods, ocean, mountain, garden, pool, or golf course, the kitchen often includes not just generous windows and French doors, but also less-familiar responses such as windows in backsplashes or see-though upper cabinets. The picture window is staging a comeback, sometimes extending down to the countertop—instead of ending at the backsplash—to grab more view. Clerestory units, installed above upper cabinets or other windows, bring in extra light and, in some cases, preserve privacy from neighboring houses.

Complex Islands

The island is now an integral part of the kitchen, individualized to the owners' needs and the overall design. Tiers, varied materials, and interesting, often curvaceous shapes redefine what was often a flat surface that dominated the room. The "obligatory box in the center of the room made of lined-up base cabinets is out," says Kelly. "The island is being treated not as a matching component, but as separate yet integral design element," he adds.

An island might look like a farm table or incorporate legs detailed to look like furniture. It might be an antique butcher block or include a circular glass section that forms an eating area. And the function is carefully integrated into design, in some cases defined by a different material and/or a variation in height, such as solid-surfacing in one area and

a cutting board in another. The island is becoming like a piece of architecture, separating the gathering area from the work space. "Often an island is used to create more intimate areas to eat and socialize in, or it acts as a divider between the living and cooking spaces," says De Giulio.

PHOTOGRAPHY: © 2001 MATTHEW MILLMAN; DESIGNED BY DOUG DURBIN

drink up!

A dedicated beverage center is an idea whose time has come. Whether a wine rack in the butler's pantry, refrigerated wine storage in an island, or a coffee bar, all reflect the dual function of the kitchen as both family center and entertainment area. Left: Designer Doug Durbin's sophisticated design serves vino or cappuccino with flair.

Hood as Hearth

With families increasingly drawn to the home in general and the kitchen in particular, there's strong interest in making the range hood a prominent, one-of-a kind design feature, whether in a contemporary or a traditional setting. Another reason for the interest in the range hood as a design element is that the advent of professional-style cooking appliances brings new attention to the cooking area, notes Kelly.

Range hoods in traditional kitchens tend to be large and hefty. They encase the cooking area, often creating an inviting, almost ceremonial hearth within the kitchen. Materials may include wood, stucco or plaster, copper or other metal, tile, or some combination of the above.

In contemporary spaces, the hood is frequently designed as an eye-catching piece of sculpture. Whether made of stainless steel—sometimes with a brushed or other finish—another metal, concrete, or tempered glass, these one-of-a-kind hoods accentuate the design of the kitchen. The hood, in fact, is often both the focal point of the kitchen and a symbol of its personality-driven design.—*Elaine Martin Petrowski*

Here's a primer on the hottest looks in kitchens across the country today.

kitchens
for the 21st century

■ The appearance of the North American kitchen may change every few years but one thing remains constant: No matter how sophisticated the look, the kitchen continues to be the heart of home. "The space still has a symbolic as well as functional role in the modern family's complex life," says Christine Mahoney, an architect based in New York City.

Mick De Giulio, of de Giulio Kitchen Design, Inc., of Wilmette and Chicago, Illinois, adds, "People are devoting more time, energy, and money to develop the kitchen because that's where they spend the most time."

The Real Living Room
That means today's kitchens are increasingly being designed as an extension of living space rather than just as a place to incorporate the mechanics of cooking, serving, and storing food, adds De Giulio.

"We're including comfortable seating groups, and even fireplaces and bookcases, to create kitchens that feel truly lived in," he says. As an outgrowth of the ongoing role of the kitchen as the center of family life, homeowners are paying increasing attention to integrating the kitchen into the rest of the home.

Let's Get Personal
There is also a growing desire to individualize kitchens. "Our clients make it clear they don't want what everybody else has," notes Fu-Tung Cheng, of Cheng Design in Berkeley, California.

Architects and designers are increasingly being asked to incorporate artwork or one-of-a-kind pieces, such as antique doors. Personalized kitchens often include built-ins to display a treasured collection or other objects d'art.

Or the design of the kitchen itself may evolve from a cherished item. De Giulio, for example, recently designed a kitchen inspired by a handcrafted Italian ceramic bowl. Other homeowners have used a piece of antique furniture as inspiration.

This new individualism has led to a fusion of styles. "It used to be that we saw French Country and English Country or contemporary styles. But now you see more personality-driven design that doesn't refer to one period or region," De Giulio observes.

"That's generated a design vocabulary with a more international flavor, exhibiting such far-flung influences as Indonesia, South America, and Mexico," adds B. Leslie Hart, a kitchen and bath journalist and a member of the National Kitchen & Bath Association's Hall of Fame.

Clean Up Your Act
Hart continues, "On the whole, the lines in today's upscale kitchens are more streamlined than they were just a few years ago." Instead of elaborate carvings and molding details, many kitchens now feature layers of texture, often created with nontraditional materials such as concrete, glass, and stainless steel.

Smelted materials such as copper and steel boast unusual finishes and patinas. Hardware and faucet finishes are moving away from shiny chrome and brass toward wrought iron, nickel, bronze, and copper.

Back to Nature
Other natural materials finding their way into the kitchen include soapstone, kirkstone, slate, and concrete for countertops. Teak and mahogany appear on counters as well as cabinets. Look also for handcrafted or recycled materials, such as glass tiles in a backsplash or heart pine flooring. While granite remains the most popular countertop choice for high-end kitchens, today a honed, matte finish often replaces the mirrorlike polish of recent years.

1. Architect John Senhauser joined a "hearth room" to a craftsman-style kitchen. **2.** An exciting mix of materials—soapstone, limestone, and granite—brings exotic flair to this kitchen, designed by architect R. Stephen Chauvin. See page 272 for this kitchen. **3.** Designer Mark Brody used color and a variety of materials for this streamlined space. See page 114 for this kitchen. **4.** Chandler P. Pierce, Jr. paired off-the-rack cabinets with components such as concrete countertops and terra-cotta floor tiles for a distinct environment.

1

2

3

4

5

6

7

8

Along with cleaner lines comes an interest in using more organic forms. Both curves and circular arrangements abound.

An emphasis on bringing the outdoors inside sometimes leads to the use of fewer wall cabinets. This not only allows the kitchen to more successfully blend into surrounding living areas, but also provides an unobstructed view outdoors. Often, an entire wall of glass floods the space with natural light. A pantry or tall cabinets elsewhere make up for any lost storage space.

The Butler Returns

Another item in big demand is the butler's pantry. The reason? Entertaining at home is perennially popular, and the butler's pantry not only provides storage, it also helps hide the cooking mess. Moreover, it serves as a staging area for drinks and hors d'oeuvres, freeing up the kitchen proper.

In a butler's pantry, designers often specify a different, but related cabinet style. Increasingly, the butler's pantry houses a sink, icemaker, base refrigerator, and wine storage unit.

It's Getting Darker

When it comes to finishes for cabinetry, there is a renewed interest in medium to dark wood tones. "Cherry, maple, pecan, butternut, mahogany, walnut, and other darker woods are popular again, but this time used with other textures and finishes to sparkle things up," says Thomas R. Kelly, of NorthShore Kitchens Plus, in Marblehead, Massachusetts. There's also a growing interest in renewable rain forest woods, such as anigre.

Jamie Drake, ASID, of Drake Design Associates, in New York City, concurs, adding, "Sometimes there's a bit of iridescence included to brighten the space." It's often in the form of wallcovering or win-

dow treatments with a slight metallic sheen or perhaps wire mesh or translucent glass cabinet door panels.

Strongly colored washes or aniline stains add depth and interest. Earth tones such as sienna and umber are popular, as are saturated deep reds, blues, or greens.

Most often these colored finishes are combined with other wood stains as an accent. For example, a barn-red aniline stain that reveals the wood grain on a center island can be surrounded by walnut or maple cabinets with a natural or tinted stain. Alternatively, wall cabinets can be finished in one stain and base cabinets in another.

Unfitted Updated

Emulating the unfitted kitchen, where a brand new space is designed to look as though it evolved over generations, it's common practice to use a variety of finishes, colors, and materials within the same kitchen. "People don't want to see yards and yards of just one material," says Kelly. "So we vary the countertop materials and perhaps include kirkstone or soapstone with granite."

Cheng agrees, noting that there's another dynamic at work, namely a "nostalgia for that which is crafted. That at least partly explains the interest in the unfitted kitchen," he theorizes.

Point-of-use refrigeration plays an important role in the unfitted trend. Rather than conform to a one-size-fits-all rigid work triangle of range, sink, and refrigerator, components are placed where they work best.

"The Sub-Zero 700 Series allows all the necessary refrigeration to be completely integrated into the space so it looks like furniture or French doors or even like the door to a closet or a wine cellar, complete with hardware," notes Kelly.

It's possible to create the look of a freestanding antique hutch that incorporates refrigeration. "Designers have a new flex-

ibility and are limited only by their imaginations," he adds. A snack area for kids, a bake zone, a breakfast area, or a salad prep area can all include concealed point-of-use refrigeration.

Light Fantastic

"Color and materials are two important tools for architects and designers to create beautiful, functional work environments,"

the latest must-have gadget

The pot filler is a cold-water faucet installed adjacent to the range that eliminates the need to hoist large pots of water from the sink.

PHOTOGRAPHY © 2001 GEORGE ROSS; DESIGNED BY JOLIE KOREK

says Mahoney, "but an important animating device is light." Proper lighting can help transform a kitchen from a utilitarian space to a romantic dining nook.

Kitchens now include a mix of lighting sources and fixture types. And designers must include a way to control the lighting to both suit the task at hand and the mood. For example, a kitchen might include incandescent ambient light supplied by recessed ceiling fixtures and decorative wall sconces that can be dimmed when dinner is served.

The same space also might include decorative halogen fixtures suspended above a prep area and indirect lighting from hidden fixtures that flood the ceiling for a dramatic effect when entertaining.—*Elaine Martin Petrowski*

---

5. Designer Shirley McFarlane dressed up a butler's pantry with handmade wood-lattice cabinet doors. **6.** In a kitchen designed by O. Franco Nonahal, sleek cherry cabinets wear a high-gloss finish. See page 74 for more on this kitchen. **7.** Kitchen designer Charlee Smith mixed woods, finishes, and hardware for a vintage look. For more, see page 160. **8.** Designer Joan DesCombes took advantage of curved windows to situate a dining nook. This kitchen is featured on page 24.

contemporary kitchens

■ Think style. Think sophistication. Picture gleaming stainless steel and sweeping curved lines. Mix in one-of-a-kind art pieces or dynamic architectural elements, and you're on your way to creating kitchens with a contemporary accent. In the following pages, you'll discover a pre-WW II New York City apartment, a '50s ranch, a new English-style two-story, and more. Their owners have used bold granite countertops, oversize skylights, and mosaic backsplashes for spunk and spirit. Add the functionality of gleaming double-sinks and convenient islands, and you'll master this exciting look so popular in every region.

Cherry cabinets are enlivened by handmade raw-steel pulls in this contemporary kitchen. Varied counter heights and the curved shape of the range hood, dining table, and seating add even more visual interest.

DESIGNER: WENDY MAYES. PHOTOGRAPHY: © GAVIN PETERS

PHOTOGRAPHY: EVERETT & SOULÉ

cool ideas!

- subtle child barriers
- grain and spice holders
- stainless-steel tambour
- circular chopping block

throwing a
curve

■ Joan DesCombes, CKD, of Architectural Artworks, faced special demands in designing a lavish kitchen for an Indian-born physician and his wife. "It's in a spectacular contemporary house overlooking the Gulf of Mexico," says the Florida designer. "The house is big, with a great many curves and vast windows—all of which are repeated in the kitchen. But the owners' primary concern was creating a design that would accommodate four young children, while simultaneously keep them out of harm's way."

DesCombes positioned an arclike raised bar at one end of the kitchen to create a dining space for the youngsters where they could also easily converse with their mother. The designer situated the cooktop on an adjacent island on the far side from the breakfast bar,

The centerpiece of the appliance wall is the Sub-Zero Model 690 side-by-side refrigerator-freezer with an in-door ice-and-water dispenser. To the left, a pullout pantry hides behind a black-lacquered panel. To the right, a tall stainless-steel tambour fronts an appliance garage. A warming drawer sits beneath the counter. Recessed halogen lights supplement pendant fixtures.

25

"The primary design objective was to accommodate four youngsters."

Above: Sized to welcome at least four helpers, the kitchen mixes steel, granite, and lacquered surfaces. Built-in glass containers store grains, legumes, and spices. Other condiments hang from a chrome bar. **Opposite:** Leather-and-steel Italian-made barstools pull up to a kidney-shaped glass-topped table. The large curved booth overlooks a palm tree-filled yard. Dramatic coastal views are to the right, beyond the family room.

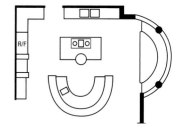

well away from the children's space. The Sub-Zero Model 690 refrigerator-freezer, built into a peripheral wall, contains in-door ice-and-water dispensers so the kids need not enter the center food prep area for refreshment. "The owners wanted all of their cool and cold storage in one place," notes the designer.

It's an American kitchen with Eastern overtones. The family's Hindu heritage is expressed in their vegetarian diet, so above the main sinks the designer provided a double row of glass-fronted pullout compartments for grains, below which a steel rail supports a long row of hanging spice vials. And despite the kitchen's opulent size—33 feet long, including a large curved booth for family dining—every aspect of the kitchen's design is focused on efficient cooking, dining, and cleanup.

Dominating one side of the island is a cooktop with downdraft ventilation; on the other is a round maple butcher-block cutting board, which tops lacquer-fronted storage for baking essentials. A vegetable sink sits in the curved work surface just below the breakfast bar. A dishwasher and trash compactor flank the main sinks. A microwave above a wall oven is handy to the refrigerator-freezer. Beside a warming drawer is a glass-fronted wine storage unit.

For dazzling durability and easy maintenance, the homeowners chose veined granite for flooring and perimeter countertops, polished black granite to top the island and breakfast bar, stainless steel for the backsplash, and lacquer finishes for the custom cabinets. "There is high-gloss black lacquer on some cabinets," DesCombes points out, "and on others a matte-finish lacquer in a seafoam-green that suggests the ocean just beyond the windows."

Cabinet hardware is minimal and convenient to use. Along with the elongated stainless-steel pulls on some undercounter cabinets, there are chamfered lips or steel grooves just deep enough to accommodate fingertip access to open the upper cabinets, and some lower ones as well. Shallow storage for cutlery and deep storage for pots and pans are located throughout the space, positioned near point of use.

A sophisticated mix of illumination allows a variety of effects, starting with indirect lighting in the multilayered step-up ceiling. Recessed incandescent fixtures line the periphery of the lowest level of the ceiling, plus low-voltage halogens serve as undercabinet lighting and are in what the designer calls "the flyover" that extends around the room, over the upper cabinets. In addition, halogen pendant globes provide general illumination in the central cooking and dining areas. "Overall, the kitchen is an efficient space with a clean, sleek appearance," says DesCombes. "It's subtle but quite dramatic, not unlike India itself."—*M.K.*

city slicker

cool ideas!

- slide-out corner storage
- flip-up cabinet doors
- concealed cutting board
- counter railings

When Pam Bradford combined two apartments into one in a New York City pre-World War II building, she had some pretty definite ideas about how the place should look postrenovation. "I wanted to mix the 'old' world with the new," she explains. "Exposing the original beams brought the apartment back to a prewar feeling. The place is very eclectic now, with our 19th-century pieces and modern paintings."

The pivotal point in making the enlarged apartment work was the kitchen, but there was some disagreement about its design. The smaller of the two original kitchens became a wet bar, and the second kitchen was to be totally remodeled. "My husband had wanted an open kitchen, but I was dead set against it," Bradford recalls. "If the kitchen, which adjoins the dining room, was open, everyone would see the mess."

She and her husband, Achilles Perry, are both lawyers—she's general counsel for Calvin Klein and he works at Goldman Sachs—and, with the help of Manhattan-based designer Yves Claude, they worked out a successful compromise. A wide pass-

through and a doorway—minus the door—help give the compact new kitchen some breathing space.

As part of the renovation, the room was slightly enlarged, although its new 7-by-14-foot dimensions can hardly be considered spacious. Claude had his work cut out for him. "You can't afford to waste space in a New York City kitchen," he says. "Everything must have a use." And so to the left of the Sub-Zero Model 561 refrigerator-freezer, a drawer incorporating a cutting board adds almost 2 more linear feet of workspace.

And, in what would normally be a dead corner to the right of the sink, the designer installed special dual-function slide-outs for corner units. "When you pull out the two-shelf unit and angle it, a second, hidden,

Right: For homeowner Pam Bradford, designer Yves Claude (standing) created a stainless-steel and marble kitchen that plays against an antiques-filled apartment. **Opposite:** Two big stainless-steel panels in the dining room above and below the pass-through are actually cabinet backs. Traditional molding on the open doorway neatly frames a view of the Sub-Zero Model 561 refrigerator-freezer.

Right: A narrow broom closet to the right of the Sub-Zero refrigerator-freezer mimics the look of the appliance.
Below: When the two-shelf storage unit next to the Wolf range is pulled out, a second hidden storage unit moves forward.

The Wolf and Sub-Zero handles were duplicated on all the cabinets.

double-shelf unit emerges," Claude notes. "It's very efficient."

Small can be good. "Standing at the range is like being in a cockpit. Everything is within arm's reach," the designer declares. And to be sure that the cook can find things easily, doors on the upper cabinets flip up and in, rather than swinging out. The doors are meant to be open when one is working so there is full access to the contents in the cabinets. Just as important, there's no chance of accidentally hitting one's head on an open door, he notes.

The sleek space is sheathed entirely in stainless steel—the designer's favorite material—with dark green marble—the homeowner's choice—on the floor and backsplash. Claude explains his passion for stainless: "Because the material lasts forever, you can refinish it by buffing it so it looks like new, and most importantly, it's 100 percent hygienic. The counters are seamless so there are no crevices to catch dirt." The professional-style Wolf range, fitted out with the grill design that Bradford preferred, blends right in.

Stainless steel also lends itself to simplicity of design, which is another of Claude's guiding principles. "Handles are the only thing we see, and in this kitchen we built the design around the Wolf and Sub-Zero handles, duplicating them on all the cabinets," he points out.

From the bold yellow dining room, the gleam of stainless steel is apparent not only through the open doorway, but also on expansive panels above and below the pass-through. The panels could be painted, but Bradford likes them just as they are. "From the dining room, the view of stainless steel and deep green marble is like a modern painting," she says. "It furthered my plan of juxtaposing modern art, which is what the kitchen is, within a rich antique setting. The kitchen is simple, clean, and beautiful. It totally works."—*Isabel Forgang*

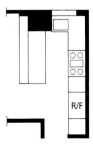

Opposite: The designer copied the handles on the refrigerator and range for the cabinets. A narrower version of the same handle serves as a railing that runs along the edge of the countertop and sink. A shallow shelf at the pass-through keeps kitchen clutter from the view of diners in the adjoining room.
Right: A cutting board set in a drawer supplements counter space.

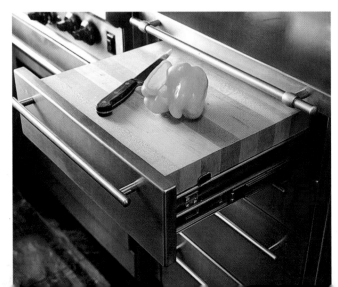

cool ideas!

■ photorealistic floor tiles
■ double-tiered upper cabinets
■ cantilevered dining table

optical allusion

■ It started out as a cookie-cutter kitchen just 7 feet wide in a New York City high rise. But when Ronnette Riley, FAIA, and project architect Mark Brungo, AIA, of Ronnette Riley Architect, got through with it, the space had nearly doubled in size. The two merged the kitchen and an adjoining dining space, creating a 20-foot-long run.

The homeowner entertains frequently. "That's why we created so much counter surface," notes Riley. The architects also removed most of the wall separating the kitchen from the living room, further enhancing the apparent size.

Part of the wall was a concrete-block structural column to which a cantilevered dining table was attached; another part was an airshaft. The architects carved out space between these two immovable elements, creating a niche for a range. "We gutted the kitchen and rearranged the components," says Riley. "Only the sink is where its predecessor had been."

The expanded kitchen exudes crisp efficiency, with its stainless-steel sink, stainless-steel-fronted refrigerator, and dishwasher, "Pietra Cordosa" stone counter, and custom cabinets faced with laminate in a stainless-steel finish. Magnetic touch latches eliminate the need for protruding handles. "Upper cabinets are two rows of square cupboards," notes Riley. "If the client has to reach something on the upper shelves, she uses a small stepstool."

The remodeled space is open to the living room, but the kitchen is defined by unique ceramic tile flooring. "The floor is fun," says Riley. Each foot-square tile is a photorealistic image of river rocks. Another fanciful touch is a pair of Phillipe Starck wing-shaped kitchen faucet handles. In this sleek cosmopolitan kitchen, function and whimsy happily coexist.—*M.K.*

Left: The compact Sub-Zero Model 611 refrigerator-freezer suits this sleek, small kitchen. **Right:** Stools of aniline-dyed bent plywood sit on chrome legs. The cantilevered peninsula is bolted to the concrete column with a steel plate. Strip lights hidden beneath wall cabinets supplement low-voltage overhead lighting.

cool ideas!

- cylinder-fronted pantry
- two-tiered island
- louvered appliance garage
- recessed cove lighting

clean
machine

■ "Simplicity was our main focus," recalls designer Timothy Vranic, of Ultimate Kitchens, in discussing the design of this ultraslick kitchen in Vancouver, British Columbia. In keeping with the overall scheme of architects Denis Arseneau and Stuart Howard, Vranic aimed for a streamlined look.

With a whole-house color scheme of black and white, a high-tech kitchen was a must. There, stainless-steel appliances play off the sheen of lacquered cabinets and polished granite countertops.

The kitchen is on the second story of the house, with superb river and mountain views, so it was imperative to minimize wall cabinets to maximize vistas and natural light.

The owners also wanted an open-plan design to encourage family togetherness. The 22½-by-25-foot space includes the family room, divided from the working kitchen by

Above: The curved pantry unit pulls open to reveal six adjustable wire shelves. **Right:** The two-tiered island terminates in a graceful semicircle: a column of brushed steel topped with granite. The Sub-Zero Model 690 refrigerator-freezer dispenses ice cubes and water. The hardware on cabinets serendipitously matches the appliance pulls.

"There are certain rules of kitchen design, but they aren't set in stone."

a bilevel island. A cylindrical pullout pantry unit inspired the semicircular treatment at one end of the 14-foot-long island. The step-up provides an innovative solution to the dilemma of where to place electrical outlets on an island. Although made of the same granite and steel that dominate the kitchen, the curved surfaces soften the other, more linear lines.

The family includes two teens, so functionality was key. "Teen-age boys hip-close cabinets and drawers," explains their mother. "We needed something that could hold up to them."

The European-style cabinets feature drawers made of steel, as are pulls and glides, and automatically close with a gentle nudge. Fortuitously, the cabinets' hardware and handles on the stainless-steel range and Sub-Zero Model 690 refrigerator-freezer look cast from the same mold.

Despite the absence of wall-hung cabinets, the kitchen boasts ample storage space. One side of the island, which includes an eating bar, provides deep drawers for utensils; on the other side, adjustable shelves hold infrequently used items. The curved-front pantry hides food staples; other nonperishable goods fill the flanking cabinets and a walk-in pantry on the wall opposite the range.

In keeping with the clean, linear elements, indirect lighting hidden behind cove molding casts a warm glow on the ceiling. Halogen spots illuminate the counter on the sink wall; graceful glass pendants with halogen bulbs over the island reiterate the rounded design motif; directional spots recessed in the ceiling handle overall lighting.

"There are preconceived rules of kitchen design for practical space planning, but they aren't set in stone," says Vranic. "You still have to listen to what the client wants." This explains the width of the aisle between the island and the perimeter cabinets.

Instead of the standard 48 inches for a space of this length, the owners opted for 42 inches. "Given the placement of the appliances, I normally would allot more space," Vranic explains. "However, in this case, the wife, the only cook in the family, wanted to be able to pivot from, say, the sink to the island and back."

The family had envisioned a utilitarian kitchen with state-of-the-art equipment and a flawlessly clean look. Such is now their reality. It is also impressive proof that clean and contemporary can be as effective as cute and cozy when it comes to making a kitchen the center of the home.—*J.M.*

Opposite: Cabinets are finished in polyurethane lacquer; floors are black granite. **Top:** The appliance garage helps eliminate counter clutter. To meet local electrical code, when the door is closed, a switch automatically shuts off power to the outlet. **Above:** Compartments organize silverware; plastic dividers lift out for cleaning.

PHOTOGRAPHY: © JOHN LINDEN

- oversize skylight
- fire-etched glass panel
- stainless-steel cabinets

sleek as
satin

■ Luxurious new cabinets were already ordered, but something still seemed to be missing in the renovation of a 1960s-era kitchen that occupies the middle level of a three-story town house in Santa Monica, California. At the eleventh hour, the retired couple decided to consult with an architect.

Douglas Teiger, AIA, of Abramson Teiger Architects of Culver City, reorganized the entire floor to create a more workable layout for both private times and entertaining. "When you are working with small spaces—this kitchen measures 8-feet-9-inches by 11-feet-5-inches—every inch counts," declares Teiger. "We ended up gutting the space of the entire floor, relocating the entry and dining room, and creating a new powder room and a new galley kitchen with a separate pantry in the former coat closet."

A key architectural feature in the kitchen is the oversize skylight, which makes the 8-foot ceilings

This all-stainless-steel kitchen is a masterpiece of surgical precision. A Sub-Zero 700 Series refrigerator sits to the right of the oven; a tambour door above conceals serving pieces. Tongue-in-groove flooring is made of maple, as is the cutting board that can slide along the counter edge. The range hood and vent take on the look of sculpture.

"When you're working in small spaces, every inch counts."

appear taller than their actual height and floods the room with natural daylight. To ensure artificial lighting did not shine directly on stainless-steel surfaces and cause glare,

Teiger placed most of the low-voltage lighting inside the white-painted skylight well in the center of the room. Two incandescent downlights over the sink and a series of small under-cabinet halogen lights supply task lighting on the counters.

When desired, the kitchen can be closed off from the adjacent dining room, thanks to an ingenious sliding panel of fire-etched glass. However, a shimmering glow through the translucent glass hints at the kitchen's powerful presence. When not in use, the glass panel disappears against an identically sized wall.

As originally planned, the kitchen cabinets, backsplashes, and counters designed by Bulthaup Kitchens of Los Angeles are all stainless steel. The coordinated Sub-Zero 700 Series tall refrigerator and freezer on either side of the wall oven fit seamlessly into the room. As a counterpart to the sleek metal, the floors are natural maple with tongue-in-groove construction. Although such an extensive use of stainless steel is more typical of a restaurant kitchen, the happy result is remarkably intimate.—*B.M.*

Top: In a process known as flaming, the fixed limestone panel to the left of the kitchen's entry was subjected to heat to make the outer layer crack and peel. Left: A translucent fire-etched glass panel slides along a track to close off the kitchen during formal dinner parties. The fixed wall to the right is surfaced in Venetian plaster.

cool ideas!

- marble toe-kick
- cantilevered glass shelves
- stainless appliance garage

PHOTOGRAPHY: © ROBERT RECK; STYLING: NINA WILLIAMS

Linking kitchen and family room is the use of cherry cabinetry, stainless steel, and Brazilian-cherry floors. Halogen lights illuminate both areas. A 68-inch-tall tower holds two ovens. The island counter is white Carrera marble.

sleek chic

■ From its clean-lined cherry cabinets and stone countertops to its stainless-steel and glass detailing, this kitchen could be in Manhattan's Soho district. It is downtown, but the city is Denver, not New York. "It projects the feel of a downtown loft," says kitchen designer Mikal Otten, CKD, of Wm Ohs Showrooms in Denver, who fitted out the space for architects and interior designers Debra Toney, associate AIA, and Mark Adcock, AIA.

"I believe that every room should have one special feature," says Toney. A cherry and stainless-steel fireplace takes center stage in the family room that opens to the kitchen. The designer-owners agreed that the kitchen wall opposite must be in balance. So Otten suggested another focal point that matches the fireplace in mass and materials: a 48-inch-wide stainless-steel Sub-Zero Model 632 refrigerator-freezer. It is surrounded by cherry cabinets finished with translucent-glass doors trimmed in stainless steel. Above, clear glass shelves seem to float, but are actually supported by sturdy stainless-steel brackets installed in the wall surfaced in the same material.

"The refrigerator wall was designed to be a focal point from the get-go," Toney says. Just beyond the appliance,

a door leads into the butler's pantry, which contains another sink and dishwasher, as well as a steam oven, wine storage unit, and china cupboards. "When we're entertaining a large group, we take the dirty dishes into the pantry and hide them and then we can deal with them whenever," confides Toney.

"Our entertaining style is usually impromptu. Our lives are too busy to plan ahead, and so we often invite groups on the spur of the moment," Toney continues. "Entertaining tends to the informal and often centers on sporting or television events such as the Super Bowl or the Grammy Awards."

The couple, partners in business and life, has six children between them. "Our entertaining varies from our two 14-year-old daughters, who live with us part-time, and their friends, to family groups, or our own friends and acquaintances," says Toney. At such times, the island serves not only for cooking, but also as a snack bar or buffet. The downdraft cooktop, which eliminates the need for a "monster hood that dominates the room," according to Otten, also allows for a clear line of sight to the large plasma television in the family room.

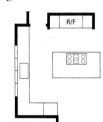

The kitchen cabinetry's furniture style helps it blend with the family room and creates "a European contemporary look," says Otten. The sleek doors and minimalist hardware add sophistication. As Otten points out, "there are no standard wall cabinets in the kitchen." A single, tall 14-inch-deep cabinet rests on the countertop on the sink wall, housing everyday glassware.

On the third wall, cabinets continue to masquerade as furniture. Here a 68-inch-tall "highboy" houses a microwave-convection oven and another electric oven. Small appliances are stashed in a stainless-steel garage tucked into the corner.

"My favorite part of the kitchen is the honed, white Carrera-marble counter," says Toney. "I love the way it wears. It becomes more beautiful as it gathers a patina." In contrast, Green Mountain soapstone appears on the counter in the sink area. The marble is used in another distinctive detail, a 9-inch-high toe-kick, as well as on the backsplash. Otten is equally satisfied. "This was a fun project for me," he concludes, "because I was given a free hand to use spectacular materials."
—*Elaine Petrowski*

Far right: The space centers on the Sub-Zero Model 632 refrigerator-freezer. **Above, from top:** An appliance garage near the sink helps keep the counter, of Green Mountain soapstone, uncluttered. Translucent-glass doors beside the fridge hide china; steel rods support glass shelves. Owner Debra Toney gets together with designer Mikal Otten.

Impromptu entertaining often centers on events like the Super Bowl or Grammy Awards.

cool ideas!

- window flush with counter
- raised "table" on island
- glass-mosaic backsplash
- pot-filler spigot over range

clearly now

■ It started out, says the homeowner, "as let's fix up a few things, and it turned into a two-year project" that converted an awkward 1970s residence in a wooded locale in Houston into a warm, inviting home. Shepherding the process were architect Leonard G. Lane, Jr., AIA, of Chelsea Architects and interior designer Marlys Tokerud, ASID, of Tokerud & Co., both of Houston.

First on the agenda was the kitchen that Lane describes as "more appropriate for a small apartment than a large house." Limited by an outside wall and an interior brick wall, he eliminated a powder room and a pantry, creating a 16-by-20-foot space. To make the most of every inch in the still compact kitchen, the space was essentially divided in half. A counter with a sink, dishwasher, and range runs along the window wall. On the opposite wall, tall cabinetry houses a built-in microwave oven, an appliance garage, china cabinet, and a Sub-Zero refrigerator and freezer.

"We chose Models 601R and 601F," says Lane, "because they provide maximum capacity in a minimal space. And clad in the same wood as the cabinets, they blend right into the wall of built-ins."

A wide island boasts specialized built-ins on three sides. "We asked the homeowners, 'how do you want to use this and what do you want to put in it?'" recalls Lane. A round, raised eating surface with a single stainless-steel support occupies one

Right: The glass of the picture window sits right on the granite counter behind the sink. The black granite floor and counter contrast smartly with anigre wood custom cabinets.
Left: Two of the kitchen's little luxuries include a pot-filler spigot above the range and a sparkling glass-mosaic tile backsplash.

PHOTOGRAPHY: FRAN BRENNAN; STYLING: JOETTA MOULDEN, WWW.SHELTERSTYLE.COM

**This kitchen rolls up its
sleeves and cleans up easily.**

end of the island, fulfilling the clients' request for a table within the kitchen's narrow confines. It also made the best of what could have been an awkward placement of the range, whose position was dictated by the window.

"We considered wall ovens and an island cooktop, but they would have seemed to crowd the island too much," says Lane. "And a hood would have been intrusive in the center of the room. The clients love this solution because they like to be able to make things and then put them right on the table."

In fact, says the homeowner, the redone kitchen "is not just the central focus of our house, it could be the only room in the house. People come in, start talking, begin eating, and never seem to leave." Function is equally pleasing. "We both enjoy cooking and really like the space. And when the time comes to get down and dirty, I must say, this kitchen rolls up its sleeves and cleans up easily."

To add warmth and beauty, Tokerud chose an elegant palette that begins with quarter-figured anigre cabinets with a clear finish. Dark, bronzy-green Uba Tuba granite surfaces the perimeter countertops and the raised table; Brazilian black granite covers the rest of the island. Black granite tile flooring and a backsplash of black glass-mosaic tiles with a pewter wash complete the high-contrast look.

"Your eye is drawn to the window wall and the mosaics sparkle in the light," says Lane. Adding illumination are glass-fronted upper cabinets that are lit from within, recessed low-voltage halogen ceiling cans, and task lighting.

When it comes to choosing the kitchen's best feature, homeowner, designer, and architect all agree on the picture window. "The one thing the lady of the house wanted was a larger window because they had beautiful views of what we call a bayou," explains Lane. "There's a smooth continuance of the counter into the window frame."

"The fixed glass," adds Tokerud, "goes all the way to the countertop so that the counter surface seems to float right through." Sums up the homeowner, "When you look outside, you would think you were in a forest 60 miles out of town."—*Phyllis Schiller*

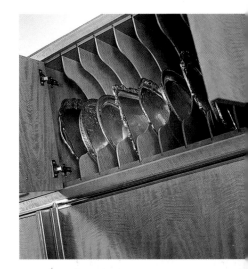

Opposite: The Sub-Zero refrigerator and freezer tuck neatly into a wall of cabinets. Frosted-glass doors access equipment in the adjoining media room. A raised table topped in Uba Tuba granite sits at the stainless-steel-clad end of an island that includes a wealth of storage.
Right, from top: Slots lined in Pacific cloth keep silver trays tarnish free; a cutting board that can also hold small appliances pops up when needed; produce pullouts are convenient to the prep sink.

cool ideas!

- wire-glass doors
- home office nook
- niches in column
- mosaic backsplash

geometry lesson

Above: The pear wood column hides a sprinkler line. **Opposite:** The Sub-Zero wine storage unit inspired the stainless-steel framed cabinets and their wire-glass inserts. The controls of the island's ceramic glass cooktop are built into the cabinet front.

■ If you plan to renovate a kitchen on the sixtieth floor of a big-city apartment building, it's handy to have a best friend who is an architect. So Chicago landscape architect Maria Smithburg called Claudia Skylar, who is in partnership with James Mastro, of Mastro & Skylar Architects.

"I know a lot about architecture but I still needed her expertise," says Smithburg. "It turned out to be a really good collaboration." She wanted the kitchen to have a timeless look that would mesh with the rest of the apartment, furnished in an eclectic mix of classic and ultramodern.

To achieve a similar blend in the kitchen, the two chose handsome, textured materials to contrast with the sleek functionality of the appliances. They opted for a warm, lush, pear wood veneer for the cabinets and "Princess Yellow" limestone for the floor. Countertops are deep green granite, and the backsplash is a mosaic of random 2-inch-square sandblasted glass tiles in a cool palette.

The apartment spans two corners of a Chicago high rise and "has more windows than walls," says Smithburg, offering sweeping views of Lake Michigan and Michigan Avenue. But the kitchen was a poor complement to the expansive rooms in the rest of the apartment. Twelve feet by 16 feet,

"Vertical lines draw the eye upward and create the illusion of greater space."

the old kitchen had a meager island that did little to encourage serious cooking and socializing.

Enlarging the kitchen wasn't easy. The room's 7½-foot ceilings concealed ductwork, and several of the walls hid immovable plumbing, sprinkler, exhaust, and electrical lines. Moreover, strict acoustical regulations dictated complicated mechanics to tile the floor—in addition to padding the dead space beneath, the tiles could not touch any walls or cabinets.

To give the room the illusion of more space, Skylar resorted to various forms of trickery. She designed the cabinets to extend to the ceiling, hiding a heating duct behind a false panel at the top. This, along with an emphasis on vertical lines throughout the kitchen, "draws the eye upward," according to Skylar.

Moving the duct from the center of the ceiling also freed up a couple more inches of height. Smithburg and Skylar agreed that another way to give the illusion of greater space was to keep the lines clean.

"Over a sink, you normally step up the cabinets to get more work room," says Skylar. "But we stepped up all the cabinets in that run." With the bottom edge of the cabinet so close to eye level, however, typical undercabinet lighting would be too intrusive. The solution: tiny low-voltage lights built into the cabinets.

Another example of Skylar and Smithburg's ability to turn a negative into a positive: When they tore down the wall to get extra space for the office nook, they discovered a sprinkler riser. Moving it was not an option. Instead, Skylar designed a column with niches that serves both as an architectural segue between office and kitchen and as a display case.

Skylar is especially proud of the subtle manipulation of negative and positive space. On one side of the kitchen, the Sub-Zero 700 Series tall refrigerator is balanced by a tall, stacked combination of television cabinet, microwave, and a 700 Series base refrigerator drawer unit. Between them, an expansive counter offers visual relief.

On the other side, this arrangement is reversed, with double wall ovens and pantry cabinets in the center flanked by counters and cabinets with wire-glass doors. "It's all engineered to mold the space," says Skylar. "It moves you in a way you can't quite describe—there's magic in the geometry."—*L.P.S.*

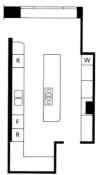

Opposite: Three Sub-Zero 700 Series units merge into the cabinetry. The tall refrigerator at the far end functions as the main appliance; the base freezer next to it is for long-term storage. **Left:** To the right of the sink, the base refrigerator stores fresh produce; above are stacked a microwave and a television—behind retractable doors. **Above:** The designer created a home office by taking down a wall and stealing a chunk of space from what used to be a dining area.

cool ideas!

- convex curved island
- wall-to-wall windows
- boldly figured granite
- circular range hood

windows on the
world

■ While this Cincinnati house was only about 15 years old, the kitchen seemed to belong to an entirely different era. When interior designer David A. Millet of David A. Millett, Inc., first visited the house, the now-flowing space consisted of two separate rooms. The windowless kitchen was walled off from an adjoining sunroom and dinette area.

Not only did the spaces seem boxy and isolated, the layout failed to take advantage of one of the hilltop home's most striking assets: sweeping views of downtown Cincinnati and the Ohio River, extending clear across the state line to Kentucky.

While the original sunroom did boast floor-to-ceiling windows, Millet notes that the room was only about 11 feet wide. "You couldn't really take advantage of the view because you were right on top of it," he says. Moreover, with all the windows, "the sunroom was almost like a hotbox."

The setup had fit the lifestyle of the original owners, who had their own chef. Meals were prepared in the strictly utili-

---

Left: The bilevel island is designed in two curvilinear segments. The rounded triangle houses the cooktop, while the semicircular seating area is organized for dining and gazing at the view. The support column beyond the glass-and-steel hood marks where a wall was removed. **Above:** The curved motif reappears in the cabinet design.

Above left: The granite's pattern plays off the curves of the burled maple cabinets. **Left:** Elongated handles of the Sub-Zero Models 601 freezer and refrigerator inspired those used for the cabinets. **Opposite:** The convex curve of the bar seating area is mirrored in the shape of the ceiling soffit. The pendant lights' metal accents also allude to the shape of the island.

"A circular shape gives a softer line, which is how the island evolved."

tarian kitchen and served in the sunroom. But the layout definitely did not work for the current owner, New York Yankees outfielder David Justice. He wanted a more relaxed and informal atmosphere when he returned to his hometown after being on the road. Justice also wanted a more contemporary attitude.

Millett's first step was to remove the barrier, creating a 15½-by-24-foot room. "Taking down the wall exposed the entire kitchen to this dramatic view. Now you can stand back and take it all in," he says. The eye is drawn immediately from the room's entrance across the space to the expanse of sky beyond the window wall.

This natural progression is aided and abetted by the sinuous island that encompasses a cooktop at the near end and bar seating at the far end. (A hidden beam and a circular support column now bear the load of the former wall.) "The design opens up the formerly square space," says Millett. "A circular shape tends to give you a softer line. That's how the whole concept for the island evolved."

The island's curved lines are accentuated by countertops of ivory-white granite. "The granite's pattern suggests motion; the more swirls the better in this case," says Millett, adding that the look is a departure from the desire of most of his other clients for a more regular pattern in that choice of stone. The illusion of movement continues in the rounded edges and surfaces of the burled maple cabinetry, and in the curving lines of the ceiling's double soffits.

Millet kept some of the basic configuration of the former rooms, placing the new sink and appliances in essentially the same locations. The decision made sense, he notes, because the interior space is still used for active prep work while the room's perimeter is naturally suited to dining or relaxing.

Because Justice entertains frequently, the side-by-side placement of individual Sub-Zero Model 601 units meets his need for plenty of refrigerator and freezer space. Their stainless-steel exteriors are echoed in the custom chrome-and-glass range hood. The glass, notes Millett, makes the hood seem to float, while allowing an uninterrupted appreciation of the view.

The kitchen's color scheme was kept neutral for the same reason. "You have the seasonal palette outside. The trees, the river, and the sky are constantly changing with the weather and the seasons," observes Millett. The only punctuation marks are the cobalt blue light fixtures that strike a perfect grace note to the colors of the sky and water on the horizon.—*Rebecca Winzenried*

cool ideas!

■ glass backsplash
■ multilevel island
■ curved cabinets
■ exposed hood duct

new point of view

Opposite: Homeowner Abby Smith (above) selected a warm autumnal palette for the family room/kitchen space dominated by a wall of windows. Brown and green tones complement the custom-made laminated-wood cabinets.

■ When builder Ron Smith, owner of Quorum Custom Homes, and his wife, Abby, a graphic artist who "finishes out" the interiors of her husband's houses, set about creating the kitchen for their new home in North Dallas, it was business as usual—almost.

"We had to make decisions quickly and keep the project on track, just as we would for any other client. Being in the business, we've learned to be decisive and not to nuance something to death," says Abby. But working with kitchen designer and cabinet manufacturer Neal Seidner, of Livingwerks Group/Salient Designs, in Lewisville, Texas—with whom they have long been acquainted—the homeowners still managed to incorporate numerous creative "nuances."

High on the couple's wish list was an interior Abby describes as "classic contemporary, but not current trendy." Because much of the day-to-day living—and often entertaining—would happen in the open family room/kitchen area, Abby selected a color scheme of autumnal colors plus purple to "play up the feeling of the outdoors and bring it inside. We chose woods and warm colors to create an inviting environment."

Separated from the approximately 18-by-20-foot kitchen space by a stepped bar, the family room features state-of-the-art media equipment. The taller of the two granite counters is 42 inches high, and the lower ledge, the standard 36 inches. The room's most dramatic aspect comes from the huge wall of windows that reveal an ever-changing seasonal show of the wooded property. "My

whole intent," says Seidner, "was to not block that wonderful backyard from any vantage point in the kitchen."

To that end, the kitchen's large island, which serves for preparing food, cooking, and eating, was strategically placed to face the family room's window wall. Incorporating not only the view but also the massive range hood by Berkeley designer Fu-Tung Cheng, as well as a glass-doored display unit, proved no impediment, thanks to a clever T-shape arrangement of 1-inch-thick tempered-glass supports.

This framework also forms the clearly practical backsplash for the 36-inch-wide Wolf range. "Unless I explain it, no one realizes that the two pieces of glass are perpendicular to each other and that they are holding up the hood and cabinet, which appear to be floating over the glass," says Ron.

One end of the granite-topped island forms a rounded eating counter that can seat up to five people. "I don't miss having a separate table," says Abby. "I have no young kids at home and this is a comfortable place for informal meals." It also works

Husband and wife share the cooking, each preparing his or her own specialities.

Right: A tall bar counter area helps to subtly delineate the kitchen from the family room. Toe-kicks in textured stainless-steel laminate complement a large column that vents the range hood and a smaller one that hides wiring. **Left:** A "floating" display unit, supported by two glass panels, stores crystal and decorative serving pieces. One of the Model 700TCI refrigerator-freezers peeks out from behind the display unit.

These serious cooks wanted the best appliances on the market.

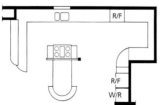

Opposite: A telephone desk tucks into a niche opposite the Wolf range. The Sub-Zero Model 427R wine storage unit is installed next to a Model 700TCI refrigerator-freezer. **Above:** A second TCI is on the sink wall. A tempered-glass structure behind the Wolf range supports the hood. Counters are Absolute Black granite, floors maple strip, and cabinets laminated wood.

well for casual entertaining, Ron points out. "We're able to serve and eat there and you can talk to the person who's acting as the chef, which in this family can be either of us."

The curving contours of the counter echo the rounded corners of the custom cabinetry, which offers stylish—and plentiful—storage. Curves are Seidner's specialty. He has the advantage of owning the high-tech plant that makes the cabinetry with all the curves and angles he dreams up. "I tell people cabinets don't have to follow walls just because the walls are there," he quips.

Seidner chose a random play of wood laminate in light and dark finishes, creating what he calls a "hopscotch-plaid" effect. (The face surfaces of the laminate are Italian poplar and an African species called Cameroon ayous. Both are cultivated using sustainable farming methods.) Stepped upper cabinets almost reach the top of the 11-foot ceiling. Lower units offer a host of storage amenities, including slide-out baskets and a pullout pantry.

Equally efficient is the choice and placement of appliances that include, along with the Wolf range, two dishwashers, a microwave, a wall oven, and warming drawers on the sink wall, with one Sub-Zero Model 700TCI refrigerator-freezer nearby. An identical unit flanks the Sub-Zero Model 427R wine storage unit with refrigerated drawers on the wall behind the island.

Both Seidner and the Smiths agree that the Sub-Zero units were necessary ingredients for efficiency. As both builder and owner, Ron extols the "flexibility" of integrating the units into the design. Abby finds that the drawers in the 700 Series are wonderfully accessible. "And the wine storage unit is very handsome and stacks bottles really nicely," she adds. "Ron loves that you can keep red wines at one temperature and the whites at another. It's a real conversation piece. People love seeing it light up. All it needs is a compact disc player and it could be a bar!"
—*Phyllis Schiller*

cool ideas!

- four pantries
- computer work station
- marquetry cabinet inlays
- stainless-steel apron

storage
galore

■ As a designer, Karen Sanders, BAAID, knows just how disruptive remodeling can be, but she also knows the pleasure derived from living in a space tailored perfectly to personal needs. So when it came to redoing the kitchen she shares with her husband, Mel, in Calgary, Alberta, she approached the project with gusto.

Opening up the kitchen to the dining room and turning it into one 22-by-12-foot area was her first priority, and for good reason. "The kitchen really is our living space," says Sanders.

Originally built in 1913 and subjected to numerous renovations during the decades, the house imposed few design restrictions on its homeowner-designer. But she did butt up against an immovable object, a chimney where she planned to place a pantry.

Sanders wanted the 24-inch pantry doors on either side of the Sub-Zero Model 561 refrigerator-freezer to echo the appliance's double-door design. Her solution

The island's stainless-steel center component follows the curve of the granite countertop. Both stand in contrast to the linear pantry units and Sub-Zero Model 561 refrigerator-freezer. The computer desk is integrated into the wall that also houses an undercounter microwave.

"Centering the refrigerator in the space inspired the symmetry of the design."

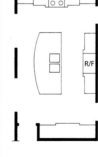

Left: A convection oven is built into the island directly across from the gas range. The range hood was designed to stretch to the cove molding. Beside the double sinks, the Bosch stainless-steel dishwasher conceals its controls in the top of the door. **Top:** Adjustable pantry shelves stow small appliances and dishes. **Above:** Zoned cutlery and spice drawers feature simple finger pulls.

was to wrap one pantry neatly around the chimney. To maintain the balance that is key to the kitchen design, the left door of the pantry to the right of the fridge is a fixed panel that masks the chimney wall. There is still plenty of storage space in the other pantries and in the wall-hung cabinets.

"Centering the refrigerator in the space inspired the symmetry of the design and became the focal point in the room," explains Sanders. "It combines the design elements from which everything else extends."

The light maple cabinetry, Verde granite countertops, and stainless-steel appliances reflect a subtle Asian influence. (Mel Sanders owns a Thai restaurant for which his wife designed the interior.) But like fusion cuisine, other stylistic influences are also brought to bear. Witness the simplified classic crown molding atop the cabinets and their marquetry inlays. And traditional French doors with true muntins provide visual relief from the minimalist cabinet style.

Italian pendant fixtures add a curvaceous component, as does the bowed stainless-steel apron on the island. Halogen spots illuminate the room at large. Smaller halogens integrate into the millwork beneath the hanging cupboards, highlighting the stainless backsplash while providing task lighting on the counter.

Sanders designed the cabinets right down to the inch. She had Cambium Millwork inlay a checkerboard of cherry and walnut into the maple cabinets around the range, refrigerator, and computer desk. By stepping the cabinets back from the range, refrigerator, and computer desk, she was able to achieve a repetitive rhythm and minimize the bulk of the cabinetry.

Placement of appliances was determined by functionality, of course, but Sanders also made every effort to keep them from intruding on her sleek design. The wall oven is placed in the island opposite the range rather than the more typical installation higher on a wall. On the opposite wall, the microwave also sits below eye level to minimize its impact on the design.

With a south-facing back yard, one dog, and two cats, Sanders was determined to relate the kitchen to the outdoors. When the couple barbecues outside, the 9-foot-long island serves as a buffet. Stereo speakers above the doors and on either side of the refrigerator provide music inside or out.

Green slate flooring adds to the indoor/outdoor motif. It is simultaneously elegant yet durable enough to resist abuse by four-footed family members. "In the summer when the doors are open all the time, patio and kitchen feel like one room," says Sanders.—*J.M.*

cool ideas!

- curved island countertop
- built-in television
- paired dishwashers
- hidden stepladders

checks in
balance

■ Turning two rooms—a kitchen plus a utility room containing a freezer, washer, and dryer—into one dramatically redesigned kitchen was only part of the challenge for bath and kitchen designer Baroque Fineberg, of Baroque Fineberg + Associates. Fineberg had to make room for the appliances he removed and create storage space lost when he eliminated a walk-in pantry. He also had to balance the Houston homeowners' desire for a state-of-the-art kitchen within a Georgian-style house.

The structural challenge required razing a nonstructural wall that divided the kitchen, then relocating the washer and dryer to a full-scale laundry room above the adjacent garage. Finally, Fineberg created a floor-to-ceiling storage wall surrounding an oven and microwave.

Installed in this wall are three tiers of cabinetry, yet the arrangement reads as a single expanse of paneling. Upper tiers are reached by means of a narrow collapsible stepladder that rolls out from behind one section of toe-kick. Two other folding ladders are concealed

Right: A Sub-Zero Model 601R refrigerator and Model 601F freezer anchor one end of the room. A pair of two-drawer dishwashers flanks the main sinks, with a warming drawer built in beside the range. **Left:** A Wolf range and hood hide a window retained for exterior symmetry. Large marble floor tiles are laid on the diagonal.

PHOTOGRAPHY: © KEVIN McGOWAN

"Transitional design uses traditional forms in a clean, but not sterile, way."

behind other toe-kick sections elsewhere in the kitchen.

To integrate the kitchen with the house's architecture, Fineberg used what he calls a "transitional" design approach, alluding to traditional forms, but using them in a clean, although not sterile, way. The newly merged kitchen space, with its gleaming stainless appliances and stained mahogany cabinets, seems timeless in design.

Cabinet design was another challenge, but meeting it earned the clients' praise and won Fineberg their trust. The clients, a couple with grown children, had collected brochures from various cabinet companies without finding anything that really attracted them.

Fineberg designed a simple cabinet door with raised stiles—to accent its verticality—with no horizontal rails. Instead of simply detailing his design on paper, he actually had a sample door built for the clients.

"Whose cabinet is that? It's gorgeous!" they exclaimed. "It's yours," he explained, but they were still puzzled. "*I* designed it," he said. "Yours is the only kitchen in the world that will have it." According to Fineberg, his gesture cemented their collaboration, confirming that all were in aesthetic agreement.

Despite demolition of the original kitchen and the utility room, the shell of the kitchen was essentially unchanged. Even the butler's pantry, with an existing undercounter icemaker, remains. "All I did," Fineberg explains modestly, "was supply new cabinetry to coordinate with the kitchen."

Arranging the elements within the approximately 14-by-26½-foot space was not particularly formidable once the designer understood how the kitchen would be utilized. "I wanted to make sure there was counter space on either side of the range," he says, "and I placed the main refrigerator and freezer units on the wall adjacent to the range." Locating a 700 Series base refrigerator in the island centralizes food prep activity so that whoever is working there has fresh produce at hand.

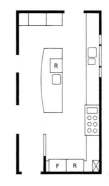

"My clients entertain a lot, and the wife is an active cook and a baker," notes Fineberg. That explains the 60-inch commercial-style range, full-size Sub-Zero refrigerator and freezer units, and two dishwashers, plus the island with its own sink, satellite refrigerator, and trash compactor.

Whether the couple is dining alone—at the island or in the breakfast room—or entertaining in their formal dining room, the kitchen is functional. Two or more people can work together, on meal preparation or cleanup, with uncluttered ease.—*M.K.*

Opposite: An oven and microwave were installed in the storage wall to look like one unit. To keep two cooks from colliding, the main sinks and island sink were placed diagonally. All three are undermounted stainless steel. **Above:** In the butler's pantry, reached by pocket doors to the right of the oven and microwave, glass-fronted wall cabinets sit over a base unit built around a bar sink and a Sub-Zero icemaker.

- two-tiered eating bar
- lift-up glass cabinet doors
- parquet flooring
- stainless-steel backsplash

jewel box

Homeowner James Tashjian (above) recently renovated his whole apartment to take advantage of the New York City views. European chestnut and glass-doored cabinets complement the granite countertop and stainless-steel appliances and backsplash.

■ James Tashjian knew just what he wanted when it came to kitchen cabinets—all the bells and whistles. What he didn't know was how to fit them into the floor plan of his New York City apartment. Clearly, he needed help in transforming the 66 square feet of his miniscule kitchen into a more workable, livable space.

Designer John Coulter of Poggenpohl U.S., Inc., didn't realize how daunting his task would be until he actually took the measurements of Tashjian's kitchen. "He was asking for a lot in a little space," recalls Coulter. "Thank heavens there were walls that could be moved and closets that could be removed."

Originally half the size it is now, the kitchen consisted of three closets but no real work areas. Without natural light and closed off from the rest of the 1,000-square-foot apartment, the space was also extremely dark. The homeowner wanted a contemporary kitchen with a combination eating/bar area that would be com-

patible with the rest of the apartment.

"Because the kitchen is situated next to the front door, it had to be aesthetically pleasing as well as functional," says Coulter. His client had already gutted and redesigned his apartment into a sleek contemporary space. Now he just needed help in transforming the kitchen.

Richly figured European chestnut cabinets and stainless-steel built-in appliances made maximum use of minimal space. The 24-inch depth of the Sub-Zero Model 611 refrigerator-freezer made it possible to include a large unit in a small space. The double-drawer dishwasher was another one of Coulter's suggestions that the homeowner applauds.

An electric oven and range top and a microwave replaced the old gas stove. "We had to do away with the gas line because of moving the walls around," comments Tashjian. "Actually, I much prefer cooking with electricity." A stainless-steel backsplash, honed-granite countertop, undermount sink, and

The owner knew that he needed help to fit in everything he wanted.

pullout pantry all contribute to the kitchen's clean, contemporary lines.

The designer utilized closed, open, and glass-doored cabinetry to keep the cabinets from overpowering the small space. The alternating flow of stainless steel and chestnut wood also helps lighten the look. "The glass cabinets have a blue tint that goes well with both the chestnut and the steel," Tashjian says. "John was able to take everything that was on my wish list into consideration and make it work."

Cabinets stop shy of the ceiling, allowing for rope lighting to illuminate the kitchen from above. Downlighting for the display cabinet, glass-doored cabinets, and countertop serves both task and mood lighting. The shallow countertop and cabinets

at the center of the U-shaped kitchen maintain a continuous flow of materials, while adding a few more precious square feet of work space.

Lighting and materials also play an important part in the eating/bar area, which transitions into the living space. Coulter suggested a two-tiered quarter circle for the bar, echoed by a correspondingly shaped light soffit above. The contractor matched the wood flooring in the kitchen area to that in the rest of the apartment, enhancing the overall cohesion of the space.

James Tashjian, an actor who goes by the name of James Caprell, divides his time between his small New York apartment and a house in Los Angeles.

Although he is used to more space in his California residence, he does not feel cramped when he's staying in his Big Apple home. That, Tashjian says, is due to the fact that, "John was able to create a kitchen area that is aesthetically pleasing as well as what any cook could want in terms of function. It also becomes a gathering place at every party."—*Barbara Dixon*

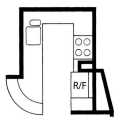

Left: A two-tiered counter opens to the dining area, which displays a painting by the homeowner. **Above:** Frosted blue-glass cabinets and open shelves keep the small space from seeming cabinet heavy. The open soffit serves as a display niche.

Above: Complementing the wood cabinetry is the stainless-steel Sub-Zero Model 611 refrigerator with a freezer drawer below. **Left:** Utensils and spices fit perfectly into one drawer; rolls of foil and plastic wrap are at the ready in another.

cool ideas!

- butted-glass walls
- stone toe-kicks
- hidden dumbwaiter
- double-layer counters

lakeside
luxury

■ The horizontal lines of this elegant kitchen echo the planes of the landscape outside a contemporary house in Bloomfield Hills, Michigan. "The open kitchen was intended to look like furniture," says architect Don Paul Young, of Young & Young Architects, who designed the hillside residence overlooking a lake for a couple of empty nesters. "Like the rest of the house, the kitchen is clean, simple, and efficient," he notes.

Kitchen designer O. Franco Nonahal, of Kitchen Studio, worked closely with the architect to design and build the kitchen. According to him, the clients wanted an elegant but comfortable open-plan space with a dining area, an island, two television sets, and a desk area. Because the two don't cook regularly, but still enjoy gourmet food, they required a lot of refrigerator and pantry storage for prepared foods.

The three-level house has a ground-floor entertainment area, which opens to a large patio. So another kitchen requirement was a dumbwaiter to ferry food and dishes up and down.

Architect and kitchen designer used various techniques to enhance the horizontal planes of the 320-square-foot kitchen. For example, a narrow band of fixed glass runs above the run of cabinets in the center of the U-shaped work area. Consistently sized cabinet drawers and doors and

Left: On the cooking wall, a clerestory window grabs light and also expresses the room's horizontal axis. Double layers of slab granite add robustness to the countertops. **Above:** The informal dining nook overlooks the lake through butted-glass walls.

"The freezer and fridge drawers help express the horizontal design."

long drawer and door pulls help move the eye in a horizontal path. A minimal number of materials and a muted color scheme contribute calmness.

"We wanted everything to be integrated, including refrigerators that don't look like refrigerators," says the designer. The Sub-Zero 700 Series, with its 27-inch width, fits perfectly within the plan. On the wall on the far side of the island, a tall refrigerator and a tall freezer, both in stainless steel, flank a base refrigerator fronted with cabinetry.

The trio ably handles chilled food storage needs just a quick step away from the island's prep sink. "The freezer and fridge drawers help express the horizontal attitude of the overall design," notes Nonahal.

The inset television sets into the cabinetry on opposing walls so the owners can keep an eye on the media no matter where they are in the kitchen. He also cleverly concealed both the walk-in pantry and dumbwaiter behind perfectly aligned cabinet doors.

For all its sophisticated elegance, the mix of materials is also completely practical. The floor is made of 2-foot-square Bottochino limestone tiles. Using the same material on toe-kicks makes the cabinets appear to float. Two layers of Tan Brown granite top the base cabinets. "One slab," says Nonahal, "is a little wimpy. Two look great." Even the seam between the layers adds another horizontal line.

Cherry cabinets wear a high-gloss polyester finish. The beauty of the organic materials is heightened by the contrast with stainless-steel appliances and brushed chrome hardware. The reflective surfaces also bounce light around, helping keep the basically windowless kitchen proper from seeming too dark.

An informal dining area overlooks the lake through full-length windows. To screen dirty dishes from diners' view, Nonahal continued the backsplash up the peninsula between the two areas, allowing for a shallow eating bar 4 inches above the work surface.

During the day, natural light floods the glassed-in dining area. Halogen spots above the island and under the cabinets, in concert with pendant lighting, provide task lighting and give a warm glow to the entire space when the sun goes down.—*N.C.*

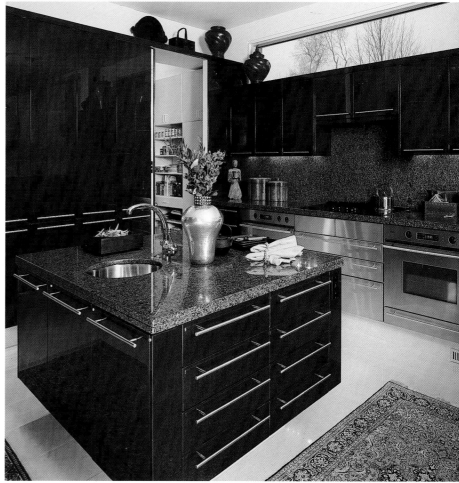

Opposite: Stainless-steel drawers of the Sub-Zero 700 Series refrigerator and freezer align perfectly with cabinet drawers. Next to the tall fridge, a 700 Series base refrigerator unit is fronted in cherry. Limestone pavers extend up to form the toe-kick. **Top:** The dumbwaiter totes food and serving pieces to the entertainment room below. **Above:** The walk-in pantry can disappear behind a door that mimics cabinet fronts.

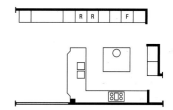

PHOTOGRAPHY: © 2002 PETER LEACH

cool ideas!

- louvered appliance garage
- extra-tall backsplash
- wall dedicated to beverages

best of
spirits

■ The occupants of this home in Rochester, New York, are as serious about wine as they are about food. As the owners of several wineries and distilleries, they felt that their kitchen had to showcase their professional and personal interest in adult refreshment. Because they are parents as well, they also needed a kitchen that would serve the needs of the orange-juice crowd. And while the house was decidedly contemporary, the owners wanted a design that was warm and welcoming.

But before tackling these challenges, kitchen designer Lorin Frye, CKD, of Willow Grove Design, in Middlesex, New York, needed to address the project's structural and spatial limitations. "There was a big wall separating the family room from the small kitchen," she explains, "which made the kitchen seem isolated."

Frye had the wall knocked down and, in the process, freed up enough space to create something the family had never had before. "Because these people entertain all the time, they were delighted to finally have a dining room," she says.

Even with the newly expanded space, however, other obstacles remained, starting with an huge skylight plunked right in the middle of the room. "I couldn't ignore it so, I had to work around it," Frye says. "The owners had wanted a big island, so it worked well to repeat the shape of the skylight. An 8-foot-long fish tank in the dining room is another visual echo."

The oversized island became both the design and emotional

Flooring and an island counter of exotic bubinga wood contrast smartly with the sleek stainless steel of the workspace. A pot-filler spigot and a rail that holds everything from tongs to tarragon ensure meal preparation convenience.

Enjoying fine wine and spirits is an important part of living the good life.

heart of the kitchen. An accomplished wood-worker, the man of the house set about crafting an island top in exotic bubinga wood. Its warm, substantial look sets the tone for the rest of the kitchen. In addition to providing seating for informal meals, the island houses a dishwasher and a prep sink.

The lady of the house had specifically requested a rail running the length of the backsplash, above the range, where she could hang utensils, condi-ments, and other frequently used objects. To accommodate the stainless-steel rail, Frye ran the custom-made mahogany cabinets right up to the ceiling, allowing for a 33-inch-high backsplash. It is clad in stainless steel to match the surface behind the restaurant-style range.

Because the ceilings were low, Frye was not concerned about sacrificing an open soffit. Still, placing the cabinets higher on the wall than usual means that they are not as convenient for storing frequently used items. Many objects in daily use, such as dish-es, are instead stored in drawers.

The wall that is adjacent to the range houses most of the appliances, including a pair of wall ovens, a warming drawer, the microwave, and the Sub-Zero Model 642 refrigerator-freezer, all in gleaming stainless steel. The door handles on the Sub-Zero repeat the shape of the drawer pulls and railing.

Of course, a kitchen is more than just a place to assemble a meal; it is also a place to savor the good life. And this kitchen pays homage to this idea with a wall dedicated to fine wines and spirits. A Sub-Zero Model 427R wine storage unit displays some of the couple's choicest bottles.

There is also a two-drawer dishwasher dedicated to wine-glasses, and an icemaker. At the far right of the wall, an opening into the dining room reveals the fish tank, creating a remarkable view to savor while sipping a glass of wine.—*Catherine Censor*

Right: One wall is devoted to fine wines and spirits. It features a Sub-Zero Model 427R wine storage unit, a dishwasher, stemware storage, a bar sink, and an icemaker. The opening to the dining room visually links the two rooms.
Above: Below-stairs bins store wine.

cool ideas!

- pass-through to bar
- built-in rolling cart
- hidden water cooler
- mirrored backsplash

steeling
beauty

■ Magnificent panoramas of Long Island Sound convinced a bicoastal executive and his wife to completely renovate this southern Connecticut house. To grab more of the stupendous view, Arlene Pilson, of Arlene Pilson Interior Design, who oversaw the redo of the whole house, bumped out the kitchen to incorporate the adjoining patio over the garage roof. The L-shaped expansion, now home to a multiwindowed breakfast room, doubled the size of the kitchen to 17 by 28 feet.

The original kitchen faced the front of the house. "The expansion opened it to sunlight and a view of the ocean out back," says Pilson. "This was the effect I was after for the entire house." She turned to Alice Hayes, CKD, CBD, of Kitchens by Deane, to implement her plan for making the kitchen as clean-lined and contemporary as the rest of the house.

"There was never any doubt about using white on the walls," says Pilson. "White doesn't compete with the

Stainless-steel appliances, including the paired Sub-Zero Model 601 refrigerator and freezer and the island cabinets of the same metal, bounce light from the adjoining breakfast room into the kitchen proper. Countertops are Absolute granite; floors are quartersawn oak.

"The less clutter and visible mechanics there are, the more the view takes center stage."

view." Stainless-steel appliances and cabinets reflect light into the kitchen's depths. "Your eye moves reflexively from the bright stainless surfaces to the view," adds Hayes.

The clients' desire to enjoy the view had only one qualification—that their entertaining needs be met. A professional-style range, double wall ovens, and Sub-Zero Model 601 refrigerator and freezer are up to the demands imposed by large catered fund-raisers the couple hosts in support of the New York arts community.

The empty nesters also appreciate the generous counter space and wide aisles during family gatherings. The new breakfast room also incorporates a fireplace.

The husband had yet another request: a station where a bartender could stand in the kitchen and pass drinks through to the dining room's bar on the other side. Pilson and Hayes collaborated on designing a removable section in the kitchen base cabinetry to comply.

The pass-through boasts pocket doors that are mirrored on the dining room side; when open, they afford a glimpse into the dining room and the view of Long Island Sound beyond. The removable base cabinet can wheel food and dishes elsewhere in the kitchen.

Achieving as much unimpeded view as possible down the length of the elongated kitchen while still keeping the kitchen separate from the formal living areas was a primary concern. Where the kitchen formerly ended, ceiling-mounted cabinets with two-sided glass-fronted doors allow light to stream well into the workspace.

"The two spaces function as a unit thanks to these cabinets," says Hayes. "One client stood at the sink underneath to determine exactly how low the shelves could be without obscuring the view."

Flush, high-gloss white cabinets on the perimeter of the kitchen and stainless-steel units on the island were Pilson's choice "for their technical precision and the way they streamline the kitchen." All are topped with counters of Absolute black granite. "The absence of textural modulation keeps the look sharp," she says.

A pop-up shelf on the island serves the mixer, blender, and food processor stored underneath. "The less visible clutter and mechanics in a kitchen," notes Pilson, "the more the view can take center stage."

The prep areas are relegated to the two back walls. The work triangle is planned for functionality but allows the cook to enjoy the view, thanks to a tall mirrored backsplash flanking the range.

Pilson credits her client with introducing the mirror idea from her other home in Malibu. Bringing the view into the kitchen was everyone's focus in this renovation, and at completion, it was everyone's joy.—*Susan Stiles Dowell*

Above, left to right: A pop-up shelf on the island keeps counters clutter-free; a wheeled cart pulls away from the base cabinetry on the one side of the pass-through to accommodate a bartender; the water cooler is convenient but tucked out of sight behind a pantry door. **Right:** Hanging cabinets have glass on both sides to welcome the view out the breakfast room windows. Purchased in Los Angeles, the wheeled table was made from movie set scaffolding.

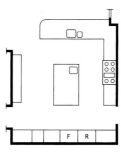

PHOTOGRAPHY: SARGENT ARCHITECTURAL PHOTOGRAPHY; STYLING: GINA COOKE-SCOTT

cool ideas!

- windowed backsplash
- flexible lighting system
- midheight storage column
- frosted-glass cabinet doors

surf and sun

■ For Penny and Wayne Lippman, the third time was definitely a charm. This sleek new space is essentially a redo of a redo. The first redo was the result of a natural disaster. In 1992, two years after the Lippmans moved into their Coral Gables, Florida, home, with its dramatic ocean views, Hurricane Andrew struck. "We had to move out of the house for 18 months while it was rebuilt exactly the way it had been," recalls Penny.

Interior designer Richard Hoffman, who had helped the Lippmans with their previous home, collaborated on the interior of this one, but somehow the kitchen got short shrift. It was the work of a cabinetmaker, who, according to Penny, made precise templates of everything, based on the original plans, and got the job done quickly.

But the kitchen proved far too traditional for a house that, in furnishings and architectural style, was distinctly contemporary. That kitchen, the owner now admits, was done, "just to get it done. Once it was finished, we knew we would have to redo it again someday."

Left: Countertops of polished stainless steel create a mirror effect, aided by light from a skylight and a cable system of halogen fixtures, including a single blue pendant. **Above:** The breakfast room, with comfortable seating that invites relaxed oceanfront viewing, complements the kitchen makeover.

Reflective surfaces pick up the colors of the ocean and sky.

That "someday" occurred recently, when the Lippmans engaged kitchen designer, Trish Myer, CKD, of Miramar, Florida, to create the kind of space they had always wanted. At that time Myer was with Poggenpohl USA in Dania Beach, Florida.

Working within the old kitchen's footprint, Myer designed a facility that, unlike its predecessor, is in absolute harmony with the rest of the house, including Hoffman's original breakfast-room plan. A limited palette of materials, all reflective to a varying degree, picks up on the colors of the sea and the sky, without competing with the magnificent view.

"The 15-by-18-foot space you see, with its pickled-ash floor and those beautiful ash-wood beams, is basically the same as before," says Myer. Topped in polished stainless steel, the island offers an ample work surface and a spot for informal dining on the other side, simultaneously zoning the kitchen into storage and work areas. Cabinets are primarily faced in brushed-aluminum laminate; a few have frosted-glass doors.

Pantry space abounds: A freestanding storage wall that stops shy of the ceiling trusses and separates the kitchen from the dining room contains a tall pull-out shelf unit for condiments and spices, plus a

Above: The stainless-steel bar sink was welded seamlessly into the island's countertop, then both were polished.
Right: A tall, frosted-glass-topped cabinet notches into the island. The tall cabinet includes a warming drawer and acts as a serving spot handy to the breakfast area. Everyday china is just visible in cabinets behind frosted-glass doors.

pair of Sub-Zero 700 Series freezer drawers, which Penny calls "incredibly convenient." In addition, tall aluminum-faced cabinets flank four square cabinets with frosted-glass doors.

"We needed a lot of storage space for dishes and glasses," notes Penny. "We chose the frosted glass for aesthetic reasons. When those cabinets are lit at night, you can sort of see into them without really seeing inside." On the opposite side of the room, mounted above the main sink and a pair of top casement windows that open from the bottom, are similar cabinets. "They present a seamless look when you stand there, gazing out at the sky and the ocean," says Myer.

Like the cabinets, each of the appliances was carefully chosen, including the Sub-Zero 700 Series tall refrigerator and two sets of freezer drawers, one on either side of the island. Myer's goal was "a total integration of appliances."

Overhead, in addition to a skylight, is a cable system hung with halogen fixtures. "We can dim them and move them around if we need to," says Penny. Most important, she says, is how the kitchen serves her cooking needs: "I absolutely wanted convenience and a kitchen with a good flow for cooking, and I got it. This is my last kitchen in this house!"—*Mervyn Kaufman*

Above: A pull-out pantry faced in aluminum laminate, with shelves for spices and condiments accessible from either side, sits beside a two-door storage cabinet with a pair of Sub-Zero Model 700BFI freezer drawers below. This freestanding storage wall separates the kitchen from the dining room.

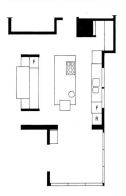

Above: Two additional Sub-Zero 700 Series freezer drawers pull out beside the tall Model 700TR to the right of the main sink on the outside wall.

cool ideas!

- buttressed wall
- commercial laminate counter
- suspended ceiling
- glass mosaic backsplash

zen complexity

■ Instead of selling the suburban home where he spent his childhood, the owner of this Bellevue, Washington, 1950s ranch decided to remodel it to gain the kind of free-flowing space typical of an urban loft. "I wanted to develop a space that reflected the way I live and the way I spend my personal time," says the owner, a 30-something bachelor. "I enjoy time alone, so the space had to be peaceful, yet I also enjoy entertaining, and it had to work for that too."

Kyle Gaffney, AIA, and his partners Shannon Rankin and Brian Collins-Friedrichs at SkB Architects revised the floor plan, eliminated walls and reconfigured the boxy rooms to create open living areas. The remodeled home includes a sophisticated but hardworking and compact kitchen designed for a client who takes classes from professional chefs and hosts groups of kindred spirits at cooking parties.

The first step in the redesign was to replace all the solid walls that previously separated the space with 4-inch-diameter steel columns. The kitchen is defined by level: It sits 6 inches above the surrounding living spaces atop a tinted concrete platform banded in steel.

Because the kitchen is visible from other living areas, SkB specified sophisticated finishing materials in a variety of textures. (Kitchen consultant Michael Chavez fitted out the cabinets and specified appliances.) Custom-made cherry cabinets feature opaque cast-glass door inserts. The panels, which resemble rice paper, obscure the contents of the upper cabinets, help lighten the mass, and provide visual interest. Pantry doors are locally crafted steel panels. Jewel-like, earth-toned recycled-glass tiles, installed behind the cooktop, are also made by a local artisan.

Though the countertops look like slate, they are fabricated of 1-inch-thick Richlite, a plastic fiber laminate. Frequently specified in commercial kitchens because it is a superior cutting surface, Richlite is so durable it is also

The melange of materials includes cherry cabinets, a commercial laminate counter, a tinted concrete floor, hand-cast glass cabinet door inserts, and a recycled glass tile backsplash. The tall 700 Series Sub-Zero refrigerator-freezer and other appliances are clad in stainless steel. The painted steel column and another framed in wood—beside a steel-paneled pantry that houses a microwave—replace supporting walls.

"We integrated appliances to avoid having them overpower living spaces."

used for skateboard surfaces and in the marine industry.

"Another challenge," says Gaffney, "was to integrate the appliances without having them overpower the living spaces." So the kitchen features stainless-steel appliances including the cooktop, oven, and range hood, and a tall freestanding Sub-Zero 700 Series combination refrigerator-freezer. Sinks, cabinet hardware, light fixtures, and bar stools are also sleek stainless steel.

The 48-inch-wide space between the perimeter counter and the island allows more than one cook to work at the same time. Other evidence of serious cooking: the pot filler behind the cooktop, two sinks, an extra-quiet dishwasher, and a 700 Series Sub-Zero two-drawer refrigerator for fresh produce, which is concealed behind base cabinet panels.

The space is dramatic at night, but during the day it is flooded with natural light, thanks to several windows, including a small one in an angled wall opposite the kitchen. Several roof windows, concealed by the suspended ceiling that forms a lid over the kitchen, "allow natural light to spill into the room without revealing the source," explains Gaffney. A narrow slice of window between the cooktop and refrigerator admits morning light and views of the landscaped courtyard and outdoor eating area beyond.

The space's ranch-house origins are disguised with some clever detailing, including a tinted plaster wall, which is sloped to catch southern light throughout the day and subtly reflect it back into the kitchen.

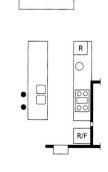

The angle also provides comfortable back support for guests to perch on a low bench while visiting with the cooks. Made of cherry to match the kitchen cabinets, it also provides storage below.

The architects also established a dynamic interplay between horizontal and vertical components. The steel beams, raised kitchen floor accented with a strip of steel, and suspended ceiling panel play off the vertical painted steel column, narrow pantry and window near the refrigerator.

For all the attention to materials and details, the owner's favorite feature is still "the way the kitchen is connected to and flows with the rest of the living space." Mission accomplished.—*E.M.P.*

Opposite: The kitchen is distinguished from living/dining areas by a suspended ceiling panel and a raised, steel-trimmed concrete floor. A cherry box set on the counter behind the main sinks holds cleaning supplies and screens kitchen mechanics from guests. **Above:** Cherry benches and a wine rack huddle around the sloping plaster wall punctuated by a recessed window.

cool ideas!

- chinese slate tiles
- light valance over sink
- two islands

natural calm

PHOTOGRAPHY: © 2002 PETER LEACH

■ A Zen-like serenity suffuses this kitchen from early morning, when it captures the rising sun's first rays, to evening, when lighting casts an inviting glow. Kitchen designer Sandra L. Steiner-Houck, CKD, of Steiner & Houck in Mechanicsburg, Pennsylvania, helped develop a design that maximizes the home's open layout and views of its wooded lot.

The owners wanted to achieve a sleek style using natural materials. "One of the most important things we achieved is the connection to the outside," says Steiner-Houck. "So when you step from the exterior to the interior, there's no real feeling of separation."

Inspiration began with the autumnal tones of Chinese slate, used for the floor and backsplash. Cherry cabinets complement the post-and-beam construction. The massive ceiling beams dictated the height of cabinets, which top out at 7 feet to align with the Sub-Zero Model 632 side-by-side refrigerator-freezer.

The addition expanded the existing kitchen space to include a breakfast area. The original, small kitchen was walled off from other rooms with a layout hardly conducive to the lifestyle of a working couple and their teenage daughter. There was "not even enough room to put a toaster and coffeemaker on the counter," recalls the lady of the house.

Steiner-Houck separated the 665-square-foot space into three work areas. "The homeowners do a lot of entertaining, so we were eager to create a big, open functional space," says Steiner-Houck. The primary island, perpendicular to the sink wall, has the range at one end and a semicircular eating area at the other.

Another island, also topped in Absolute Black granite, with a curved insert of teak, houses a prep sink and warming oven. Guests can sit at the dining table and gaze through the kitchen and breakfast room to the woods beyond.—*Rebecca Winzenreid*

Right: The Sub-Zero Model 632 refrigerator-freezer's doors overlaid with cherry panels blend with the cabinets. The island's curved doors house serving pieces for the adjacent dining room. **Left:** The two-tiered dining area of the main island suggests a sushi bar and allows diners to communicate with the cook. Floors throughout the house are made of Chinese slate in "Earth."

contemporary in color kitchens

■ Contemporary has traditionally meant chrome, glass, and black—the starker the better. Happily, today's new contemporary look is being lightened and brightened with unexpected bursts of color and vibrant personal mementos. In this section you'll discover the popular palettes today's homeowners just can't resist—from hint-of-mint green to passionate purple and rockin' retro red, yellow, and blue. Add a few hip touches like glass backsplashes, halogen lighting, and streamlined columns and you can color your kitchen with contemporary flair.

Sherbet colors and stainless-steel appliances create a Euro-style kitchen with a cool and classy feel. On the peninsula adjoining the breakfast room, large windows throw cheerful light into the kitchen. See page 110 for more on this kitchen.

DESIGNER: FRIEDEMANN WEINHARDT; PHOTOGRAPHY: © TED YARWOOD

cool ideas!

■ inlaid terrazzo floor
■ coordinated counter
■ custom pot rack
■ computer desk

smooth moves

■ For years, the hillside lot was considered unbuildable because of its steep slope and the fact that it was blanketed with up to 30 feet of bad fill. But Seattle architect Clint Pehrson, of Clint Pehrson Architects, and his wife, Maggie, took a chance. "It needed a pretty dynamic foundation to put a house there," he recalls. This foundation now supports a 5,800-square-foot contemporary house built on three levels, each one just a room or two deep—so that most rooms, including the kitchen, have a sweeping view of the city skyline and the storied Space Needle.

"Our kitchen really is the heart of our home," Maggie believes. "It's where we have family meals and entertain our extended family. There's a desk there and a computer, so it's also our mail station and a place where our two boys can do their homework."

With walls that are a combination of cinder block, which also extends to the exterior of the house, and quartersawn maple, which was used on all the custom cabinetry, the kitchen is light and bright. What gives it a special flair are the personalized terrazzo countertops and floor.

"Jack Mackie, an artist friend of ours, designed the floor," says Clint. "He knows us well enough to create a variety of images that reflect aspects of our life." Dancing is one of

Opposite: The pot rack above the butcher-block-topped island and a rail system behind the range keep frequently used utensils at the ready. Pendant lights almost disappear among the pots and pans. Cinder-block walls that comprise the exterior also make an interior appearance. **Right:** Clint and Maggie Pehrson take a dance break on the custom terrazzo floor.

This kitchen is used for dancing and homework as well as cooking and eating.

them. Prominent in Mackie's floor design are dance steps he created from templates of the shoes Clint and Maggie wore on their wedding day. With these shoes, says Clint, Mackie "invented a dance that never existed before."

Mackie used synthetic terrazzo, which was troweled on in sections separated by zinc strips. "Our terrazzo was a mixture of epoxy matrix and an aggregate comprising chips of marble, granite, and glass, plus mother of pearl," the architect goes on to explain. "There are other images on the floor, too: a moon, a sun, and a great quill pen that evolves into a conch shell. Then the whole pattern jumps

up on to the countertops and continues there," he adds.

Terrazzo is the only unusual material used in the 16½-by-18-foot space, which also features glass and stainless steel, in addition to maple. "Our everyday glassware and stoneware are stored in glass-fronted cabinets that make the entire space feel a little more open," says Clint. To keep Maggie's most-used cooking vessels in full view, he designed a pot rack that hangs above the island. He also specified an elegant rail system that extends across the range wall. "That keeps all the prep tools out where they can be seen," he continues. Adds Maggie, "We don't have

Above: A Sub-Zero Model 700BR refrigerated drawer unit tucks into the island, accessed by satin-finish stainless-steel pulls that influenced the choice of similar cabinet hardware.
Right: The primary refrigerator-freezer, a Sub-Zero Model 632, is built into a pantry wall along with a microwave and a television.

drawers full of a lot of things you have to hunt through."

Clint assists in the kitchen, but Maggie is the family cook, and it was she who selected the appliances, including a Sub-Zero Model 632 side-by-side refrigerator-freezer and Model 700BR refrigerator drawers. "It's a handy arrangement," says Maggie. "When I'm cooking or working at the island, I don't have to walk around the room to get something from the big refrigerator."

Opting for a professional-style range necessitated also installing a high-powered hood to exhaust cooking odors and heat. "That one moves 1,500 cubic feet per minute,"

marvels Clint. He installed an equally powerful heat exchanger, which pulls in outdoor air by means of a roof-mounted fan. This unit recovers heat from the house's heating system to warm the outside air coming in, then returns it to the kitchen through a grate above the hood.

The space is a delight for Maggie to work in. "Clint and I actually use the kitchen at the same time—and we're still talking," she jokes. And no matter what she is doing, there's always a dazzling city view to distract her. "Because of that view," she confides, "we've had people volunteer to come over and do the dishes!"—*Mervyn Kaufman*

Above: A pair of Maggie's dancing shoes stands among the ethereal swirls of Jack Mackie's floor design. The same terrazzo is also used on countertops. **Right:** The counter embracing the main sink steps down to form a desk top with a computer and mail station. Beyond it, "Divided Light," painted by Susan Bennerstrom, hangs on the wall.

cool ideas!

- bistro table
- striped tile floor
- stepped cabinets
- aubergine walls

color on the line

■ Bold colors and an eye-popping striped floor may be the first things that visitors notice in this Oregon kitchen. But behind the dramatic color scheme and sophisticated mix of shapes is a comfortable and highly functional space that allows owners Nawzad and Laura Othman to hang out with their frequent guests.

In the roughly 10 years the couple had lived in their home on Lake Oswego, just outside Portland, they had never been happy with the kitchen setup. They had worked with interior designer Karol Niemi, principal of the Portland firm that bears her name, on the rest of the residence. The kitchen was the last and most complex project that Niemi tackled. "The house is compact, but the kitchen is particularly petite," she says.

In approaching the project, Niemi's first priority was to gain breathing room, while replacing the appliances with models that could fulfill the homeowners' desire to take "function to a whole new level." The kitchen was originally a narrow galley

Right: The line of ochre tiles on the floor acknowledges a wall that was removed to gain valuable space in the remodeled kitchen. **Left:** Interior designer Karol Niemi (far left) and homeowners Nawzad and Laura Othman enjoy one of Oregon's regional wines at the bistro table attached to the peninsula.

The bistro table has become the social center of the kitchen.

with a wall separating it from a utility area. "We were able to capture some of that space," the designer says. "It makes the kitchen feel twice as big, even though it's not." The space measures barely 200 square feet.

The plans required general contractor Paul Grimstad of Grimson Company, in Tigard, Oregon, to reconfigure an existing stairway. He built the step-down into the utility room level with the kitchen floor. The reclaimed space allowed installation of a Sub-Zero Model 424 wine storage unit. A microwave above and undercabinet lighting help create a bar setting that's a magnet for guests. "It has worked out marvelously. Even though the wine storage unit is at the back of the kitchen, people don't have any trouble finding the wine," jokes Niemi.

"Although the house has a formal dining area, there are just the two of us," explains Laura, "so we didn't want to eat all our meals in the dining room." So Niemi replaced a slap-dash breakfast bar with a peninsula that works as both a work counter and bistro table. "This took the function to a whole new level," Laura says. "People like to gather around the peninsula while I'm cooking. It can seat four people comfortably. Even though the stove is right behind, it's become the social center of the kitchen."

The Othmans originally considered having two ovens. But with space at a premium, they opted instead for a Wolf 36-inch-wide professional-style range. "The range is sized generously enough that we have as much cooking space as we would with a second oven," says Laura. "We have even taken to using it for grilling seafood instead of firing up the outdoor grill." The Wolf's design also allows the graphically bold backsplash to flow uninterrupted. "Many professional-style ranges have rather unattractive wall protectors," adds Niemi.

Indeed, upon entering the kitchen, one's eye is immediately drawn to the cooking area by the stripes of Absolute Black granite and white Thassos marble tiles on the floor. The floor was, in fact, one of the first choices the homeowners made, having admired a similar one in Niemi's office. "A lot of people ask, 'don't the stripes make a small space look smaller?'

Left: The striped tile floor draws all eyes to the Wolf gas range, whose signature red knobs are echoed in the color of the chair backs. **Above, from top:** The aniline-stained cherry wall cabinets display varying depths and stair-stepped heights; ochre limestone tiles join Absolute Black granite and white Thassos marble on the backsplash; the peninsula's edge and brushed-stainless cabinet pulls introduce curved shapes in the primarily linear design.

The bar area with its wine storage unit is a magnet for guests.

But I think it's just the opposite. They really open it up," says Niemi. She paired the design of the floor with a complementary backsplash of the same materials, but varied the proportions. "I don't like anything too matchy, matchy," she explains. On the backsplash, the ochre limestone predominates.

"The kitchen has a sense of humor," Niemi continues. "There's a level of wit that eliminates the seriousness that often comes with modernist statements." To soften the visual impact of the black-and-white stripes, she rounded the edges on the peninsula and stained the cherry cabinets a warm claret with multiple layers of aniline stain. Aubergine-painted walls pick up tones used in the living room, into which the kitchen opens, artfully linking the two areas.

For the owners, the kitchen's striking looks make it the focal point of the house, but what excites them most is how well the kitchen works. "It looks beautiful, but it's also extremely functional," says Laura. "It's really an unbelievable transformation."–*Rebecca Winzenreid*

Reconfiguring the space allowed room for new appliances. Removing the wall separating the kitchen from a utility area (a remnant of the wall remains) created the perfect spot for a stainless-steel Sub-Zero Model 650 refrigerator-freezer, while a Sub-Zero Model 424 wine storage unit and a microwave now occupy the space that once housed a staircase.

Using solid surfacing for the island counter allowed its edge to be built up, then chiseled for a handcrafted look. The L-shaped floor plan makes the most of limited space, creating ample work surface and storage for cookbooks.

green
scene

■ When Liisa Matson of Metro Design remodeled a 1970s kitchen in a contemporary-style home in Columbia, South Carolina, two cooks turned out to be a good thing.

"Andrew and Susan Duncan knew exactly what they wanted," recalls Matson. The two own Cucina, a local gourmet food and culinary accessories store. In addition to cooking for pleasure and entertaining, the couple uses their kitchen to test new recipes and products.

"The room's architecture was nondescript," says the designer. "The 250-square-foot space had low ceilings and no focal point." The clients wanted a commercial-style cooktop with

cool ideas!

- chiseled counter edge
- free-form island
- stainless backsplash

separate double ovens, so Matson made the cooktop and hood the center of the design. "We tied the two together with the stainless-steel backsplash, then set the cooktop on cabinets of the same metal to distinguish them from the other units." The Sub-Zero Model 632 refrigerator-freezer and double ovens (not shown) anchor each end of the room.

The bold color of the matte lacquer cabinets became another prominent feature, in counterpoint to maple flooring and countertops and birds-eye maple bookshelves. At one end of the island, a maple cabinet conceals the prep sink plumbing and a trash container. "The Duncans wanted a sense of openness, so we decided to keep the island's base open and use a stainless leg at the other end as a support," explains Matson.

"We didn't want the kitchen to be square and boring," says Andrew Duncan. To create some funkiness, we had a 'chipping party.' Friends chipped away at the island's solid-surfacing top until we got the degree of funkiness we were looking for."

The indentation in the island also has a practical purpose: "It helps Susan and me to work comfortably without running into each other."—*B.D.*

The sculptural island offsets the solidity of the stainless-steel cooktop and hood, wall ovens, and the Sub-Zero Model 632 refrigerator-freezer. The maple base of the island conceals plumbing and a trash container.

cool ideas!

■ lacquered cabinets
■ stainless-steel backsplash
■ hidden microwave
■ double dishwashers

in the lime light

■ How do you turn a space of approximately 200 square feet into a welcoming, contemporary room? You devise a hardworking layout and select utilitarian materials carefully—then for surprise and excitement, you add color!

When this busy family with two teenage daughters relocated from Great Britain to Ottawa, they purchased a new but traditional English-style home. The oak kitchen was hardly in keeping with the owners' love of color and playfulness; nor were they willing to forgo the contemporary look they had enjoyed abroad. Another mandate when they met with designer Friedemann Weinhardt of Design First Kitchen Interiors was for a space that would allow two cooks to work comfortably at the same time.

Storage, as in any compact space, was also an important issue. "We wanted an extremely functional kitchen with clean lines and a modern twist," comments the homeowner. "Basically we were looking to replace the existing kitchen with one with European styling."

The kitchen is without direct natural light, sitting between a breakfast area/family room with large windows on one side and the

This Euro-style kitchen blends sherbet-colored polyurethane lacquer cabinets by SieMatic, stainless-steel appliances, and solid-surfacing countertops. Even the pendant lights conform to the cool color scheme. On the peninsula adjoining the breakfast room—whose large windows throw light into the kitchen—two dishwashers wear cabinet panels.

formal dining room on the other. According to the designer, the homeowners wanted a color that "feels like summer, suggesting buds and plant stalks." They used a paint swatch of Pratt & Lambert "Shy Green" to get the right color of matte lacquer polyurethane on the SieMatic cabinetry. The hint-of-mint color enhances the natural light borrowed from adjoining areas.

Two dishwashers and a Sub-Zero Model 700 TCI refrigerator-freezer, plus a 700 Series base refrigerator, are fronted with cabinet panels, achieving a clean look. On the cabinets, long, stainless-steel pulls, like those on the refrigerators, serve as the only ornamentation.

The team selected stainless steel for the ovens, cook-top, hood, backsplash, and sinks, citing its utility and appearance. "We chose the solid-surfacing countertop for its uniformity, clean lines, and overall contemporary look," explains the owner. "The very European color and stainless steel produce a unique blend," notes the designer.

Recessed halogen lighting positioned over the center island and undercabinet spots provide plenty of artificial illumination. Pendant lights maintain the sleek, Euro look. According to the homeowner, "The ubiquitous microwave had to be accommodated inside an upper cupboard to the left of the range because Friedemann and I could not find anywhere aesthetically pleasing to place it."

Every square foot of space is used optimally. As the

Above: The Sub-Zero 700 Series base refrigerator by the prep sink is designated for fresh produce. **Right:** On the pantry wall, pullouts flank the tall Sub-Zero Model 700 TCI refrigerator-freezer. **Far right:** Double ovens both open from the side. The island is close enough to use as a set-down area for hot pots.

"The very European color and stainless steel are a unique combination."

owner says, "The island is great for both preparing and serving food." Both sides are outfitted with refrigerated drawers, pullout containers for recyclables, and narrow cupboards for glassware, vases, and pitchers. On one wall, tall pullout pantry units access food staples and other ingredients.

"Of course, we would have preferred a larger space," she adds, "particularly with longer work surfaces, but the kitchen makes the most of the existing space, and there are no long walks for us. The floor plan allows a smooth transition from preparation to serving to cleanup."

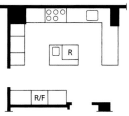

The peninsula that separates the kitchen from the breakfast area/family room houses a pair of dishwashers, which comes in handy when the family entertains. To mask the view of dirty dishes from guests seated in either the breakfast area or dining room, the adjacent stainless-steel sink and drain board are tucked in the corner—well out of sight.

In the breakfast room, the cabinet's color reappears in the chairs' upholstery. The oak strip floor that runs throughout the kitchen, breakfast room, and family room contributes continuity and makes the kitchen proper appear larger.—*Barbara Dixon*

cool ideas!

- lacquered cabinets
- open shelves
- base cabinets on legs

true blue

What is missing in size, this bright blue stunner of a kitchen makes up in attitude. Despite its 10½-by-15-foot configuration, it has plenty of room for food preparation, storage, and dining. Most clients in space-starved New York City apartments stack cabinets to the ceiling. "These folks were different," recalls kitchen designer Mark Brody, CKD, of Kitchen Solutions, Inc. "They asked for a kitchen that felt roomy and spacious."

To achieve their aim, Brody limited the number of wall cabinets and extended them up only 7 feet in the 10-foot-high room. He also raised the base cabinets off the floor on legs instead of using a toe-kick. A 6-by-4-foot pass-through links the kitchen to the dining room, enhancing the feeling of spaciousness.

Brody's clients are both doctors and the parents of two young children. The couple enjoys color and selected the

Efficient yet playful, this kitchen maximizes storage with a combination of cabinets and open shelves in blue lacquer, chrome, stainless steel, and natural maple, all manufactured by SieMatic. Lower cabinets perched on stainless-steel legs add airiness.

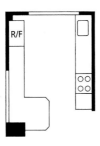

Top left: Pots and pans stash in deep drawers in the base cabinet. **Left:** A two-tiered cutlery tray doubles the capacity in this drawer. The tray was ordered from the cabinet manufacturer and fits in a standard-size drawer. **Opposite:** A pass-through behind the L-shaped granite countertop overlooks the dining room. The Sub-Zero Model 650 refrigerator-freezer slots into space at the end of the counter.

"A galley kitchen is one of the most efficient, with plenty of counter space."

dramatic hue for the matte lacquer-finished cabinets. The color sets off the maple, maple-look laminate, and stainless steel that comprise the other materials in the room. Befitting their analytical frame of mind—she is a pediatrician; he is an internist—the couple mapped out how they would work in the new kitchen. The space was meticulously planned to extract the utmost performance from every square inch. "Everything in this kitchen is there for a reason," says the designer.

His design sets up two lines of opposing cabinets and counters. "The galley kitchen is one of the most efficient, with few steps from one major appliance to another and plenty of counter work space," he explains.

Actually, this is a modified galley, thanks to the continuation of one counter into a table that forms the short end of an "L." The table also serves as an auxiliary preparation center. A walk-in pantry on the other side of the room provides plenty of storage for food staples.

If the room's size is modest, its elements are grand, including top-of-the-line cabinets by SieMatic. In addition to the blue-lacquered cabinets, Brody specified open shelves and glass-fronted lift-up units in maple, as well as open shelving of chrome wire. Countertops are Verde Maritaka granite from Brazil. A light green base with beige veining, the stone is a fine counterpart to the brilliant blue-and-maple cabinets.

Several different materials are used for the backsplash, including the same granite, a maple-finished laminate, and stainless steel, which extends from behind the range all the way up the wall. Oak flooring contributes warmth.

Stainless steel is used in other decorative and functional ways. The range, a dual unit with an electric oven and a gas cooktop, mixes black glass and stainless. The hood is also stainless steel, as are the Sub-Zero Model 650 refrigerator with a freezer drawer at the bottom, pulls on the cabinets, and legs of the base cabinets.

Lighting consists of halogen pendants mounted on a track that winds around the room. Suspended fixtures can be moved and adjusted on the track. But in practice, Brody says, most people arrange the lights once and then never make any changes. Of course, when you have planned as meticulously as this designer and his clients have, changes are rarely necessary.—*B.M.*

cool ideas!

■ fold-up cabinet doors
■ hammered-steel backsplash
■ cantilevered glass eating bar

bold and
blue

■ "An urban oasis," was the mandate that homeowners Rob and Maureen Rose gave designer Friedemann Weinhardt, of Design First Kitchen Interiors in Ottawa, when they needed help planning the kitchen of their new townhouse. Rob, a software executive, and Maureen, a landscape designer, had found that over the years their design style—reinforced by trips to New York City, where they had seen innovative interior design in restaurants—had progressed from country charm to urban sophistication.

This shift in sensibility prompted the couple's move from their large Victorian home. The original plan of the townhouse called for a small eat-in kitchen, which didn't suit the family's culinary needs. Both Rob and Maureen cook, and one of their two teenage daughters aspires to be a chef.

The priority, Rob explains, was "a good-sized kitchen that was extremely functional" and would accommodate family and guests while the couple prepped a meal. They also required good storage, in addition to a display area and a place for a computer. To make room

Left: Maple cabinets and bold color temper the coolness of stainless steel, glass, and honed granite. The curved ceiling soffit alludes to the curve of the island. **Above:** The 65-inch-tall oven tower steps down in height from the neighboring wall cabinet; the small desk eases the transition to a window.

for everything, Rob says, they were willing to do without a table in the kitchen. Weinhardt picked up on the Roses' vision for a clean-lined, contemporary and, above all, efficient space.

Fitting the couple's dream kitchen into the house's open plan proved challenging. The main level contains 728 square feet, of which the kitchen would occupy 290. Moreover, a railing open to the foyer below and tall windows meant that only two walls were free for cabinetry and the couple's long list of equipment needs. To integrate living, dining, and kitchen areas—and guided by the Rose's love of contemporary design—Weinhardt conceived of the three spaces as one, using a combination of sweeping curves and unified materials.

Having only two walls to work with, Weinhardt settled on a basic L-shaped kitchen plan, enlivened by a gracefully curved island. Placement of the Sub-Zero Model 680 refrigerator-freezer determined the kitchen's work triangle. The island houses the prep sink and the cooktop. The designer was able to squeeze in an amoeba-shaped glass eating bar, ideal for snacks or breakfast. Another unusual feature is the 65-inch-tall tower located on one leg of the "L" that houses the oven, a plate warmer, and a cappuccino machine.

Maple cabinets with slab-style doors and finished with a Chianti-color stain integrate well with the stainless-steel appliances, pulls, and other trim. Adjoining the oven tower, hinged glass and wood cabinets lift up for easy access and keep the wall unit from seeming oppressive in volume.

"In contemporary design," Weinhardt explains, "less detail is better." The Roses endorsed that idea. "We didn't want anything busy for the cabinets," says Rob. "I mentioned hammered stainless steel and Friedemann came up with the idea of using it on the backsplash. He also suggested the honed-granite countertop." The combination of wood, stone, steel, and glass was then carried over into the dining area and living room.

Lighting was paramount to the design. Weinhardt installed task and mood lighting, delineating the various work zones. The design of the ceiling soffit mimics the curved center island. A pendant light is situated over the curved, glass eating bar, which cantilevers over one end of the island. Rob chose the final bold feature—the cobalt-blue walls.

Maureen sums up her pleasure with the new kitchen in a few words. "We knew what we wanted and Friedemann knew how to make it come alive."—*Barbara Dixon*

The couple loves to cook, and one of their daughters is an aspiring chef.

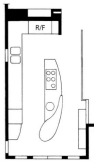

Right: The Sub-Zero Model 680 refrigerator-freezer blends into the wall of maple cabinetry. A hint of cobalt blue occasionally peeks through a hammered-stainless-steel backsplash. Counters are made of honed granite, the floor of oak strips. **Far left:** The lower halves of the lift-up cabinets are fitted with frosted glass; the doors stay put until lowered. **Left:** A pull-out pantry beside the refrigerator stores staples.

cool ideas!

- lava-stone counter
- hidden pantry
- illuminated backsplash
- floating light bridge

island treasure

■ When Kiyoe and Koji Minami first came to him with plans for their new house in Honolulu, the kitchen left much to be desired, recalls kitchen designer Troy Adams, CKD, president of Studio Becker, with offices in Honolulu and Los Angeles. The couple, with four-year-old twin boys, felt that the relatively small, enclosed room wasn't conducive to their lifestyle. "I wanted the kitchen to be open to the living and dining rooms so I could watch my kids while I'm cooking, and so I could join in the party when we're entertaining," says Kiyoe.

Fortunately there was still time to amend the plans. The first step, says Adams, was to remove two walls and set the kitchen on an angle to both the living and dining rooms. "And because the adjacent rooms had so much glass frontage, we were able to eliminate the window in the kitchen and maximize the storage here," he adds.

Placing the kitchen on an angle freed up enough space to incorporate a laundry room and walk-in pantry. The floor plan refers to the space as a "hidden pantry," and that is exactly what it is. To the left of the stainless-steel Sub-Zero Model 642 refrigerator-freezer is a pull-out vertical pantry. Next to the pullout is a similar full-height cabinet door, but open it, and instead of the interior of a standard

Stainless-steel appliances, including the Sub-Zero Model 642 refrigerator-freezer, and a pair of stainless-steel appliance-garage doors provide visual relief to the expanse of cherry cabinets. Low-voltage halogen pendant fixtures play up the brilliant glazed finish of the Pyrolave lava-stone island counter.

The capacious island is ideal for making pizza with the children.

24-inch cabinet that you would expect to see, you walk into an 8-by-12-foot room that's tucked behind the refrigerator wall. It holds a washer and dryer plus plenty of open shelving.

With the kitchen exposed to the rest of the house, Adams suggested an interesting mix of visually stimulating materials, including concrete, lava stone, stainless steel, frosted glass, and cherry, which appealed to the homeowners. "The design footprint of the kitchen was relatively simple, so we put the emphasis on the materials. If you put a lot of emphasis on details and have a busy layout as well, the result can be chaotic," he explains.

The most visible—and unusual—material in the kitchen is also the element Kiyoe likes best—the turquoise-hued lava-stone counter on the six-sided island. "Lava stone, quarried in France from dense volcanic rock, is sliced into slabs, polished, enameled, and fired in an oven. It's nonporous and scratch-, stain-, and heat-resistant," the designer says, ticking off its desirable properties.

But for the homeowner, the most important quality is the lava stone's size. "I love to make pizza with my kids and their friends and the big island is very useful for that," says Kiyoe. "It's also great for the buffet parties we like to have." The color choice, Adams notes, was inspired by the ocean.

The Pyrolave lava stone reappears as a shelf above the stainless-steel cooktop. The remaining counters and backsplash are concrete, chosen for its earthy look, in counterbalance to the gleaming lava stone. The large expanse of natural cherry cabinets adds warmth to the room and picks up on wood tones elsewhere in the house.

Adams shaped the island to allow for a conversation spot when friends and family gather round. The angular shape of the island is echoed in wood above it.

"Most people overlook a ceiling treatment," says the designer, "which leaves the room looking unfinished. We wanted something clean and simple, so we mirrored the shape of the island with a wood shelf and floated it so it would not appear boxy." The stems of pendant halogen light fixtures pierce the shelf, adding to the airy feel of the kitchen, where a mood of casual comfort prevails.—*Isabel Forgang*

Above: The frosted-glass backsplash behind the curved glass and stainless range hood can be backlit for drama. The shape of the light bridge mirrors that of the island. **Opposite:** Glass shelves over the sink feature angled steel bars, each containing three 10-watt halogen bulbs that light a collection of Japanese porcelain. An aluminum track inset into the concrete backsplash holds a rack to allow dishes to drip-dry over the sink.

cool ideas!

■ unusual color scheme
■ lift-up glass-fronted doors
■ table built into island
■ organization center

purple
reigns

■ Not everyone wants to retreat to the suburbs! This residence in the heart of downtown Baltimore offers both urban energy and a suburban-style back yard. The house was built within the shell of a former nine-car garage.

This sleek kitchen is part of a 1,000-square-foot combination space that serves as the main living area of the two-story house. It opens onto a tranquil, brick-covered private courtyard.

"On a beautiful day when you're outdoors in the courtyard, you don't even hear the sounds of traffic," says architect Rebecca Swanston, AIA, of Swanston & Associates, who happens to live on the same street.

In the kitchen, the stimulating color scheme is the first thing that grabs your eye. Wood cabinets boast a purple aniline stain; solid-surfacing countertops are cool-as-a-cucumber pale green.

"The purple adds whimsy and originality," says Swanston. "When one of the clients said her favorite color was purple, and what did I think about using that color for cabinets, I said 'terrific' because it's a large space that can readily handle a strong color."

Both husband and wife took an

Opposite: At the ceiling, sandblasted glass-fronted cabinets handle overflow storage. The granite-topped keyhole-shaped island accommodates a second sink and recycling bins. The Sub-Zero Model 632 refrigerator-freezer anchors one end of the open-plan kitchen. **Above:** Two full-size ovens and a 48-inch cooktop ease food preparation.

127

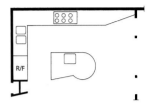

active role in the kitchen's design. His architectural millwork concern built the cabinets. As a former professional chef, she did considerable research to select the right appliances, finally settling on a 48-inch cooktop and two full-size ovens.

The 48-inch-wide Sub-Zero 600 Series refrigerator-freezer meets her demands for generous capacity and excellent performance. As an architect, Swanston appreciates the sleek, flush exterior of the Sub-Zero unit with its stainless-steel front, which integrates

well into the contemporary space.

A mix of other materials contributes top notes. The island, for example, features an "Uba Tuba" granite countertop with a circular table built in at one end. Stainless steel reappears on the ovens, range hood, and backsplash.

The island's maple base cabinet provides another visual counterpoint. It accommodates a second sink as well as storage for recyclables and other waste. The flooring throughout the house is porcelain tile that suggests slate.

To handle the owners' large *batterie de cuisine* and serving pieces, cabinets stretch to the 11-foot-high ceiling. What look like clerestory windows of sandblasted glass around the perimeter of the room are top-hinged storage cabinets. They mimic actual clerestories used throughout the house.

The glass fronts also serve to break up the mass of the wood cabinetry below. The somewhat inaccessible cabinets hold items used only occasionally. For now, they can be reached with a stepladder. Eventually, a railing and moveable library ladder will make it easier to retrieve items.

The homeowners are a young couple with three kids and a busy lifestyle. "There are always people at this house and they congregate in the kitchen," says Swanston. The seats of choice are the handcrafted stools at the rounded end of the keyhole-shaped island.

The island is strategically placed to make socializing easy while at the same time limiting access to the work triangle of the kitchen. Another key to efficiency is an organization center that includes a desk, telephone, and bulletin board. Shelves above the desk accommodate an extensive collection of cookbooks.

The brilliant color scheme helps this kitchen stand out. But the architect was careful not to allow it to overpower the rest of the open-plan living area. The end result is a kitchen that offers both delight and efficiency.—*B.M.*

Above: The dark green granite island top contrasts with the pale green perimeter counters. Metal-framed French doors set into a windowed wall lead to a courtyard with brick walls. **Opposite:** The organization center is the command post from which this busy household operates.

"When you are outdoors in the
courtyard, you don't even hear
the sounds of traffic."

cool ideas!

- bilevel island table
- pulldown upper shelves
- wheelchair-accessible sink
- side-opening oven

in the best
circles

■ The design of this colorful, semicircular kitchen in Clinton Township, Michigan, was dictated largely by the special needs of its owner, Christopher Grobbel. Confined to a wheelchair because of a spinal cord injury, he needed a kitchen that was fully accessible. Fulfilling the adage that stringent challenges bring about the best design solutions, the kitchen is a cheerful, functional, and well-ordered space. It is a comfortable work environment for Grobbel, who enjoys gourmet cooking, as well as for his wife, who handles day-to-day meals.

The couple wanted the kitchen to be the heart of their new home. "For me, the kitchen is important in that it serves as a sanctuary, a place to unwind from stress," says

Designed to accommodate its wheelchair-bound owner, the kitchen has a circular floor plan reiterated in the shape of the island and the lighting fixture. The range hood is another sculptural form. The island's two tiers welcome both bar stools and a wheelchair. Cabinets are finished in high-gloss polyurethane. Vinyl floor tiles mimic granite but are safer underfoot.

Grobbel, owner of Action Wood Technologies, a firm that designs residential floor plans, furniture, and accessories—all of which follow the principles of universal design. He planned the 600-square-foot kitchen with the help of Joe Evola of Star Cabinets, who laid out the project and built the cabinets.

The semicircular plan has a round central island that works also as a kitchen table for the couple and their son. With no corners to turn, the shape makes for easy wheelchair maneuverability between counters, appliances, and storage areas.

However, achieving the circular design, which has an 18-foot radius, was a challenge for the cabinetmaker. Evola found himself in a position to empathize with his client. "Ironically, I was temporarily in a wheelchair at that time, due to a foot injury," he says.

To make the cabinets follow the curve, he built them in increments of 27 inches with 1½-inch fillers mitered at 135 degrees. All counters are black granite. To enable Grobbel to access the hanging cabinets, Evola used shelf mechanism hardware that lets the entire shelf unit pivot down. "Because my wife is not very tall, she finds this arrangement extremely practical too," notes Grobbel.

When it came to appliances, the Sub-Zero 700

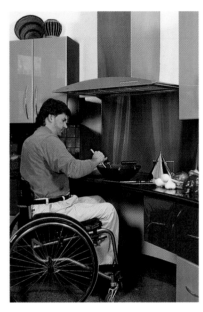

Above: Roll-under cooktop allows Christopher Grobbel to cook with ease. **Top center:** Pulldown shelves store condiments at point of use. **Top right:** Both freezer and fridge in the Sub-Zero 700 Series feature easy-access pullout drawers. **Right:** Behind the desk are eye-level windows. **Opposite:** Kohler's wheelchair-accessible roll-under sink has high-radius corners to minimize spills. The 27-inch cabinets have narrow filler units mitered to follow the curve of the black granite counters.

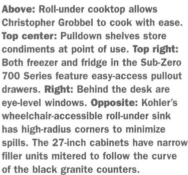

"The kitchen serves as a place to unwind from stress."

Series refrigerator and freezer were the obvious choice. The 27-inch width dovetailed perfectly with the width of the cabinets, while the pullout drawers on the bottom were convenient for use from a wheelchair. "They are phenomenally functional," says an enthusiastic Grobbel.

Both the sink and cooktop were installed with roll-under space to promote accessibility. A side-opening oven is also convenient—he can roll right up to it without having a bottom-hinged door get in his way.

With these technical considerations under control,

Grobbel aimed for a streamlined look, in keeping with the overall look of the house. He also wanted it to be fun place. Accordingly, cabinets wear a high-gloss urethane finish and anodized chrome fittings. The reflective surfaces are mirrored in the island's steel base.

Glossy gray 18-inch-square vinyl tiles form a dramatic floor pattern. A large red-and-gray pendant light fixture over the central counter and artwork on the double-height walls above the cabinets add playful touches. "You won't find another kitchen like it," says Evola with pride.—*Nayana Currimbhoy*

PHOTOGRAPHY: ALAN WEINTRAUB, STYLING: SUNDAY HENDRICKSON

cool ideas!

- ■ mix of hardware
- ■ art-glass cabinet doors
- ■ each wall a different color
- ■ conical steel hood

serious fun

■ Inspiration for kitchen design can strike at any time or place. For Anita Cole and Canice Wu, it came, appropriately enough, during dinner. The couple, parents of three youngsters under the age of five, had recently purchased a house in San Mateo, California. "We knew we wanted a very special space that was kid-friendly but highly functional for gourmet cooking," recalls Cole. "We didn't want a commercial look, but were at a loss for how it should look. Nothing was really jumping out at us until we had dinner at Circo, in the Bellagio Hotel in Las Vegas. Suddenly we realized that we wanted a kitchen with the ambience of a restaurant, a fun place where people like to be."

It wasn't just the inviting atmosphere that inspired Cole and Wu: The lively circus theme, with its bold colors and whimsical designs, puts everyone in a good mood. The couple was so impressed that they

Left: The island was designed as an art piece to soften the otherwise rectangular lines of the kitchen. A conical range hood is installed above a wall of cast glass. Art glass and mirrored panels enliven the upper cabinet doors. Colorful pendant lights over the island "resemble cotton candy, but don't shout circus," says designer Lou Ann Bauer.
Above: Homeowner Anita Cole surveys her playful domain.

Design inspiration came during dinner in a Las Vegas restaurant.

sent their designer, Lou Ann Bauer, ASID, of San Francisco-based Bauer Interior Design, to dine at the restaurant so she could get a sense of it firsthand.

"The idea was to have a 'big top' feeling without being corny. We used color to get the feeling of action and excitement," explains Bauer. The cabinets, for example, mix maple, sycamore, and paint-grade wood. Color stains highlight the grain of the maple and sycamore, while a sage glaze provides a solid field of color on the

remaining cabinets. Doors of wall cabinets are brightened by either fused-glass panels crafted by a local artist or iridescent colored mirrors. Satin nickel hardware adds to the room's sense of playfulness. "None of it matches. I used somewhere between 12 and 15 different knobs and pulls," notes Bauer.

Continuing the lively theme, each wall is painted a different color: sage, butter-cream, blue, and orange. Behind the sink, a colorful mix of diamond-shaped ceramic tiles set in a random pattern forms a vibrant backsplash; a sheet of glass with a yellow cast protects the wall behind the cooktop. Bauer chose glass, she says, because "Anita uses a wok a lot and I wanted something that would be easy to keep clean." Countertops offer still more eye candy. An unusual figured blue granite circles the perimeter of the room, while the free-form island is topped in avocado-green solid-surfacing with a raised cherry-wood eating bar.

Although Cole refers to the kitchen as "a big play room," a lot of serious cooking takes place there. "We'll have 16 people for dinner, and I can get a lot of food done at one time," she says. With a pot-filler spigot above it, the rangetop welcomes big pots of soup and stew; its wok burner also gets a lot of use. A two-burner ceramic-glass cooktop in the island handles reheating of food as well as preparation of such dishes as risotto, which require delicate heat control. Beneath, a warming oven helps with plating food. The island also houses a sink and dishwasher, as well as Sub-Zero 700 Series refrigerated drawers. "That's where I keep all my vegetables, and it's perfect for prepping," says Cole.

The U-shape perimeter wall houses a Sub-Zero Model 650 refrigerator-freezer, the primary sink, and two dishwasher drawers installed side by side. The focal point of the room is the huge conical hood, designed by Fu-Tung Cheng of Berkeley, California, made of steel with brushed and swirled finishes. Windows that provide a view of redwood trees frame the hood.

Although the kitchen is bright and colorful, it's soothing too, says Cole, "because of the way the colors are integrated with the woods. It's a fun place to be."—*Isabel Forgang*

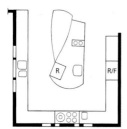

Far left: The circus theme extends to the dining area, with its drum-base table, and climbs right up the stairs. **Left:** Four-inch-square wood inserts in contrasting finishes border the maple-plank floor. **Opposite:** The Sub-Zero Model 650 refrigerator-freezer, like the adjacent cabinets, hides behind a colorful mix of painted and stained wood.

- refreshment bar
- jalousie window backsplash
- diner-style banquette
- concrete snack counter

retro revival

■ What can make swimming and sunning at the shore even more fun? In this case, grabbing a snack back at the house! Bob's Big Boy, an 8-foot-tall statue that once beckoned diners from the roof of one of the 1950s hamburger joints of the same name, invites good times and great snacking in this Ocean City, Maryland, beach-house kitchen. The homeowner, who is the CEO of the restaurant chain Kahunaville, purchased the vintage signage years earlier from a franchise that was going out of business.

Memories of summers in the area led the homeowners to buy an oceanfront lot. But what motivated them to start building their dream cottage was putting Big Boy front and center in the kitchen.

Staging the space around Big Boy's brash style was the challenge faced by the designers. The team included Pietro Giorgi, Sr., CMKBD, of Giorgi Kitchens & Design in Wilmington, Delaware; consultant Ellen Cheever, CMKBD, ASID, also of Wilmington; and interior designer Gregory Gorrell of Kennett Square, Pennsylvania. "We knew the clients loved pop art and advertising memorabilia," says Cheever. "They like traditional architecture outside, but they want interiors that burst with color and vitality. At the beach house, we had the license to be even more daring than at their primary residence, which we also worked on."

Gorrell started the process by working a 1950s-style

Opposite: An 8-foot-tall Bob's Big Boy sign brings a retro mood to a beach-house kitchen.
Above: The refreshment bar behind a stainless-steel tambour door is near the concrete-topped snack counter but well removed from the serious cooking area at the far end of the kitchen.

Zoned refrigeration serves both serious cooking and serious snacking.

Opposite: Big Boy's outfit inspired the checkerboard motif of wood and acrylic cabinet panels. Similar panels cover the two Sub-Zero Model 650 refrigerator-freezers to the right. **Above:** The sink area affords a beach view through a conventional window, a backsplash of retro jalousie windows, and glass-backed wall cabinets. **Right:** The Sub-Zero Model 700BR refrigerator, stocked with fruit and juice, caters to snackers—outside the main traffic flow.

feeling into a practical layout for the vacationing family. "I wanted to treat the kitschy commercialism of Big Boy as sculpture by literally putting it on a pedestal," he says about the idea he and Giorgi conceived to station the figure over a dining banquette, where it could be seen from the kitchen, dining, and family room.

"I used Big Boy's colors and checkerboard motif on the cabinets," Gorrell adds. A combination of solid-colored acrylic door fronts and translucent stains on wood moderate the palette, and top-quality craftsmanship and materials refine the commercial theme. Plenty of stainless steel is a 1950s diner touch. Showing up in the range hood by Berkeley, California, designer Fu-Tung Cheng, it delivers a sculptural counterpoint to Big Boy. A wall of iridescent glass mosaic behind the hood plays off the steel's reflective surfaces.

The need for spatial organization was as important as the retro look. "All the rooms were planned around views of the beach," says Giorgi. "Getting that kitchen window in the right place, then maximizing the view, was important. We used wall cabinets with glass fronts and backs on either side of the window, and a backsplash of retro-style jalousie windows below."

The lady of the house "wanted to make refreshments accessible to her children and guests," Giorgi adds, "yet put them far enough away from where she would be cooking so people weren't traipsing through her work space." The result is a clever separation of work and fun: At the kitchen's far end, a rangetop, pizza oven, two dishwashers, and a pair of 600 Series Sub-Zero refrigerator-freezer units are at the ready for meal prep.

When family or guests come in for breakfast or a snack, they need go only so far as the kidney-shaped, concrete snack counter near the kitchen's entrance. Underneath, fruit, snacks, and beverages await in the Sub-Zero Model 700BR two-drawer refrigerator. Opposite the counter, behind a stainless-steel tambour door, is a fully equipped refreshment bar stocked for breakfast and round-the-clock use.

The snack center is a godsend for Mom. Big Boy, a beacon for the hungry, might be saying, "Anything goes at the beach, especially the great American pastime of snacking."—*Susan Stiles Dowell*

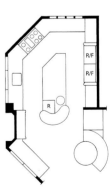

country kitchens

■ If this style still brings to mind pastel collections of cutesy bunnies and ribboned, ruffled window treatments, the pages ahead will delight you! Today's country looks are as varied as the kitchens you'll discover in this section. From new-age cottage looks to Tuscan flavor and Arts and Crafts accents, these kitchens interpret country with unique surprises. The weathered barn plank flooring and bright jolts of color prove this isn't your mother's "country."

Maple cabinets painted a creamy white and decorative muntins add an informal, cottage-style feel to this kitchen that serves double duty as one of this family's favorite gathering places.

DESIGNER: BETSY HOUSE. PHOTOGRAPHY © JEFF MCNAMARA

cool ideas!

- honed-granite countertops
- acorn-adorned brackets
- beaded-board paneling
- "subway" tile backsplash

white
is right

■ White kitchen cabinets are often dismissed as sterile and cold. But the new owners of this Georgian-style home in St. Louis, Missouri, preferred the pristine color scheme for their renovated kitchen. With the help of designer Chris Berry, ASID, of brooksBerry & Associates, Ltd., in St. Louis, white proved the right way to give the new space a bright, airy charm.

But let's back up a minute. Although the house was only five years old, the new owners (who had bought it from the builder) felt that the kitchen did not display the level of quality and detail appropriate to the house. What began as a simple replacement of the original white laminate countertops progressed to include changing the laminate cabinets, and before long, had morphed into plans for a major renovation. Nonetheless, both designer and homeowners agreed that very little structural work was necessary.

"Even though the house is rather formal outside, the decor is really soft," says Berry. To carry that feeling into the kitchen, she seasoned the white-on-white plan with a variety of warming touches, such as retaining the original hardwood flooring and adding deep dentil crown molding at the ceiling.

Berry chose honed granite in Tropical G for the counters for its resemblance to the soft blue-green color of soapstone. But

---

The 6-by-4-foot island sports a five-burner cooktop and prep sink. The renovation centered on retaining the side-by-side Sub-Zero 600 Series refrigerator and freezer, which are fitted with white-painted panels that echo the cabinet fronts.

A smart remodeling brings a builder's kitchen up to speed.

unlike soapstone, which requires oiling that gradually darkens it, granite will retain its light color. The marine hue is echoed in the pale blue-green walls. Berry added other touches suggestive of seaside architecture, such as the beaded-board island base with a counter supported by acorn-adorned roof brackets and upper cabinet doors with divided-light glass panes.

"The use of the Sub-Zero refrigerator and freezer were among the smart things the builder did," says the homeowner. "We worked around them. I absolutely love them. They're big, which is great. When it comes to storage, if you've got it, you use it." The panels on the Model 601R refrigerator and 601F freezer match the doors of the custom-built wood cabinets.

The new island includes a generous 16-by-18-inch prep sink. Storage accessed on both sides and ends eliminates any wasted space. The main sink, of gleaming stainless, sits beneath the kitchen's original windows, which overlook 33 acres of woodlands owned by the Missouri Botanical Gardens. Double trash bins tuck into cabinetry to the right of the sink; to the left are the dishwasher and an icemaker.

The breakfast area, on the other side of the kitchen, is defined by a change in ceiling height: It soars from its normal 10 feet to 18 feet, where sliding glass doors lead out onto a deck.

Originally, a two-person desk occupied one entire wall in the breakfast room. The space has been put to better use with a desk that is just large enough to hold a computer, which gets a lot of use with two teenagers in residence. Beneath the desk a drawer pulls out to reveal the computer's printer. To soften the look of the generous desk and draw the eye upward, Berry topped the pediment with a pineapple finial.

Fulfilling an item high on the owner's wish list, the vacated space now houses a china hutch. To keep clutter under control, drawers below the hutch hold linens.

Even though this kitchen renovation expanded dramatically from the original plan, the homeowner has no complaints. "We did the kitchen, laundry room, and half bath," she recalls. "It grew like crazy, but we're glad it did now that it's over and done."—*Janet Cappiello Blake*

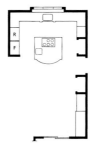

Opposite: The desk's pineapple finial is a classic symbol of welcome. The hutch holds a treasured china collection. **Top:** Divided lights of upper cabinets suggest a seaside cottage. **Above, left:** Roof brackets help support the granite countertop. **Above, right:** The brushed-nickel faucet matches drawer pulls and hinges. "Subway" tiles, a throwback to turn-of-the-century kitchens, form the backsplash.

PHOTOGRAPHY: © JESSIE WALKER ASSOCIATES, STYLING: AURELIA BUELL

cool ideas!

- saw-tooth detailing
- kirkstone counters
- resurfaced vintage sink
- glass-fronted range hood

island
romance

■ Her children like to grab food on the run; his kids are used to meals made with fresh ingredients. The owners of this Chicago-area home, a couple who had blended their families for a total of four youngsters, had very specific—if very different—needs regarding the renovation of their kitchen. They called on architect-designer Lisa McCauley to resolve these conflicting desires, even as they prepared to adopt two more children.

The renovation of the kitchen in the 1950s-era house was already under way when the homeowners turned to the principal of McCauley Design in Barrington, Illinois. The space had been opened into an adjoining dining room to form a roughly 17-by-19½-foot room.

However, the owners didn't feel that their concept for a mix of nontraditional materials was coming through in the original architect's plans. "The materials related more to a contemporary look, which wasn't what we envisioned," says the husband.

Fortunately, despite their differences regarding function, the couple shared a

Left: A pro-style range defines the kitchen's primary work area; the cabinet to the left houses a Sub-Zero 700 Series tall refrigerator. Antique stained-glass panels and a clock were built into the range hood. The 6-by-4-foot island topped in kirkstone stands on robust legs like a piece of furniture. **Above:** The saw-tooth design was inspired by the trim on an antique cupboard.

"The kirkstone looks like it's been there for more than a 100 years."

similar design aesthetic. "They were looking for a very warm, old-world style—a kitchen that looks as though it has been well lived in," recalls the designer. The husband also expressed a desire for the unfitted, furniture-style cabinetry that reminded him of kitchens he knew as a child in Europe.

Inspiration came from an antique pine cabinet that the wife had bought. This in turn provided a solution for one of his requests. "He wanted a commercial-style range," says McCauley. "But that presented a challenge because the large appliance definitely has a presence. We really only had one wall where we could put it."

She seized the opportunity to bring the family's conflicting styles together in this area, and it in turn established the style for the whole room. The range is flanked by what appear to be painted pine cabinets, which actually house Sub-Zero 700 Series units—a tall refrigerator on the left side, and a base freezer unit on the right.

Pantry shelves above the freezer drawers hold grab-and-go foods. (The microwave is located in the island, opposite the sink, just a couple of steps from the freezer-pantry.)

McCauley ornamented each unit with saw-tooth detailing copied from the

antique cabinet. At the center, the range hood hides behind a pair of antique English stained-glass windows. Set in panels, they are backlit for maximum effect. (The panels can be easily removed for cleaning or to change light bulbs.)

The large island sits on what McCauley describes as "fat opera singer legs." It is topped with kirkstone, an English slate, selected in lieu of granite for its no-sheen, well-worn look. "It looks like it's been there for more than a 100 years," she says. The same goes for the slate tile floor. The designer was on site while the tile was being set and dropped in smaller, tumbled pieces for a random effect.

To allow one person to clean up while another is cooking, McCauley placed the sink and dishwasher along the wall to the right of the freezer drawers. Kirkstone is also used for this full run of counter. The vintage English farmhouse sink, which was resurfaced with new porcelain, is another example of how the mix of old and new elements works in together, much like this blended family.—*R.W.*

Below, left to right: The desk sits between a cereal pantry and the antique pine china cabinet that influenced the kitchen's cabinetry—now painted linen-white to match the other cabinets. Radiant heating under the slate tiles allows youngsters to play on the floor without getting chilled. A pantry tops the Sub-Zero 700 Series base freezer; narrow pullouts on either side of the range hold spices.

cool ideas!

- ■ luminous glass tile wall
- ■ top-hinged cabinets
- ■ banquette eating area
- ■ integral drainboard

new-age
cottage

■ After living in their early 1900s Arts and Crafts-style cottage for four years, Eileen Marolla and Chuck Sterne were ready to tackle the outdated kitchen. They turned to their friend Jamie Swidler, a Philadelphia designer, to help them incorporate new cabinets and appliances without making any major structural changes. Swidler's strategy was to divide the roughly18-by-14-foot room into zones and maximize the efficiency and visual appeal of each area.

"The kitchen had cabinets and an electric range that dated from the 1960s. And aesthetically it was just not up to speed with the rest of the house," says Swidler. "The other rooms are very elegant."

"Our main goal was to put in a gas line for a cooktop and add a new Sub-Zero refrigerator-freezer," adds Marolla. She had an older side-by-side Sub-Zero but wanted one with the freezer on the bottom. "I love to cook with fresh ingredients," she says, "so I rarely use my freezer."

The new refrigerator became a design catalyst that

Factory-made cabinets occupy the main work zones. Custom maple display cabinets are lit from within with halogen lights. The stainless-steel drainboard and sink were custom made as one unit. The room's focal point is a mosaic made of Vitria glass tiles by California Art Tile. The counter under the mural serves as a buffet for casual dinner parties.

"When you sit at the table, you see the garden reflected in the glass tile mural."

resulted in a palette of stainless-steel appliances, soapstone countertops, and white cabinetry for the utility zones. One wall serves as the storage zone, housing the fridge and closet-sized pantry units.

Opposite is the cooking zone, with the cooktop and stainless-steel oven, sink, and dishwasher. "It's an atypical configuration of the 'work triangle,' but it works well for Eileen," explains Swidler.

"Before the remodeling, when you were sitting at the kitchen table, you'd see that awful range hood and overhead cabinets and a dishwasher," continues the designer. She increased the kitchen's elegance quotient with a glass tile wall, glass sconces, and a maple banquette.

Although Swidler specified manufactured painted-maple cabinets for the main work spaces, she had open shelves and display cabinets, fitted with glass doors and interior lighting, of solid maple made by a local cabinetmaker.

"When you sit at the table you face the glass mural—a visual focal point of interest and beauty," adds Swidler. Below the mural, made of 10-inch-square glass tiles, she created space to set up a buffet dinner, perfectly suited to the couple's style of entertaining.

The designer also maximized the room's prime architectural feature with a sitting area beneath the bay window. "Prior to the remodeling, the wall under the bay came straight down to the floor," she notes. "So we knocked out the sill and created a banquette. Even though it was a matter of just a foot and a half, it makes you feel much closer to the outdoors."

Marolla had been somewhat concerned that the kitchen would turn out to be too contemporary, admitting, "The mural was a little over the top for me, but now I think it's the best part of the kitchen. When you're sitting at the table, you can even see the garden reflected in it. It's an incredible space." —L.P.S.

Top right: The designer chose the palette for the glass mural but the owner designed the pattern. Soapstone countertops have a honed finish. **Right:** The Sub-Zero Model 650 boasts a freezer drawer beneath the refrigerator. Pullout drawers and a run of top-hinged doors maximize pantry storage. **Far right:** Custom woodwork in natural maple warms the dining nook. Glass-tile sconces on either side of the bay window echo the mural on the opposite wall.

form follows
function

■ Can you spot the design concessions to physical limitations in this kitchen in Duluth, Minnesota? If not, Rebecca Gullion Lindquist has achieved her goal: To design a kitchen to accommodate the needs of a woman with multiple sclerosis without compromising style.

"Too often an accessible kitchen yells 'handicapped,'" says the designer, "with recessed areas under the sink for a wheelchair and appliances installed at a lower level. Whenever you enter the room, you're reminded of the disability."

Measuring 12-by-17 feet, the original kitchen of the 1940s-era house was decently sized, but was an ergonomic nightmare. Cabinet doors were sliders; sink, refrigerator, and stove all huddled in one end of the room. Foot traffic from the garage cut through the kitchen. A vinyl floor, poor lighting, and garish red walls added aesthetic woes.

Lindquist took her initial design cues

The owner requested 16-gauge stainless-steel counters like those found in hospitals for ease of maintenance and germ resistance. Sub-Zero's Model 650 stainless-steel refrigerator adds more gleam. Its freezer drawer is easy to access from a wheelchair.

from the building's strong horizontal lines, with its flat roof, narrow brick siding, and strip windows, selecting flat-paneled cabinets with doors that echo an Arts and Crafts theme. Moldings on top of cabinets and on the tray ceiling reinforce the horizontal thrust.

The client is almost 6 feet tall and still able-bodied, so the kitchen must work now at her eye level. Still, the room may one day have to accommodate a wheelchair. For the present, one of the few special needs was for the owner to be able to access items and appliances without painful stooping.

The semicircular peninsula can be easily modified in the future to become a wheelchair-height workstation. Two ovens allow the same flexibility. The client now uses the wall oven; the commercial-style range with oven would be more useful if she becomes wheelchairbound. The Sub-Zero refrigerator-freezer is user-friendly right now. The homeowner finds its handle easy to grasp and the 24-inch-deep interior allows her to easily find what she needs.

Because she experiences hypersensitivity to touch, as well as occasional numbness in her fingers, textures and tactile sensations became an important consideration as well. Cabinets of satiny smooth cherry wear a natural finish. The homeowner tried dozens of cabinet pulls before finding a style that did not require her to curl her fingers. To eliminate the potential for injury while rummaging  through drawers, Lindquist designed a peninsula-wide knife block. Utensil rails on the backsplash put other kitchen tools within reach.

Lindquist revised the traffic flow to make it easier for a wheelchair to maneuver. The wide pantry allows access to the majority of stored items. Two sets of French pocket doors lead from the kitchen to the dining room, easing the flow at buffet dinner parties. Because her client is sensitive to both noise and light, Lindquist provided a cork floor to soften footfall and general kitchen clatter. The tray ceiling also absorbs sound. All lighting is on dimmers and a soothing shade of celadon green colors the walls and ceiling.

While paying careful consideration to her client's present and future physical needs, Lindquist did not forget to cater to her spirit. She referenced her art pottery collection with a backsplash of metallic-finish ceramic tiles. "It's the perfect marriage of form and function," marvels the delighted client. "I have the most ergonomic kitchen imaginable, but it also has high aesthetic values."—*C.C.*

Above: In the dining room, French pocket doors to the kitchen suggest shoji screens. A Japanese tansu cabinet holds a collection of 1930s art pottery. **Right:** The peninsula contains a prep sink, knife storage, utensil storage, and seating area. The peninsula can be cut down to wheelchair height if necessary in the future. Above the bulletin board, a louver hides the television.

cool ideas!

- ■ unfitted cabinets
- ■ retro-look tile
- ■ "checkerboard" floor
- ■ concealed microwave

variety
show

■ Cabinets that look like individual pieces of furniture topped the wish list of the family—a couple with two children—that owns this newly renovated 16-by-16-foot kitchen. The home, situated in West Jordan, Utah, is only 20 years old, but the owners wanted the kitchen to suggest a vintage many decades older.

Designer Charlee Smith, of Peppertree Kitchen & Bath, pulled out all the stops to fulfill the owners' desire for variety while creating a space that is both functional and visually cohesive. She not only employed several woods and finishes to distinguish individual cabinets or groupings, but also varied heights and even the cabinet hardware. Peppertree built all the cabinets.

The alder wall and base cabinets surrounding the sink are painted white, while knotty alder units around the cooktop and next to the tall pantry sport a distressed-and-glazed wood finish. Red paint distinguishes the full-height pantry and a black stain on the cabinetry that houses the

Beaded-board wainscotting and moldings frame the cooktop. The entire arched area is surfaced with rectangular white tiles reminiscent of those used in the early 20th century. Cabinets flanking the cooktop are made of knotty alder. The Sub-Zero 700 Series tall refrigerator pretends to be an old-fashioned file cabinet.

"The look of the refrigerator could only have been achieved with the Sub-Zero 700 Series."

tall Sub-Zero 700 Series refrigerator, both on clear alder.

Door styles are equally varied. Some of the white wall cabinets have solid doors with simple recessed flat panels; others sport insets of textured, antique-looking "water glass." Drawer and door shapes and sizes are varied in continuous runs, as well as from one grouping to the next, to extend the illusion of individual pieces accumulated over time. Some half dozen decorative hardware styles range from porcelain knobs to simple metal rings.

In stark contrast to the clean-lined white cabinets near the sink, a tall black box reminiscent of an old wood filing cabinet, complete with file lock escutcheons and bin pulls, houses the refrigerator. "The original plan was to use a 42-inch-wide Sub-Zero 600 Series refrigerator-freezer," recalls Smith. "Instead, I suggested the slimmer Sub-Zero 700 Series all-refrigerator unit along with a separate base freezer unit. The look could never have been achieved with another brand."

Another sleight of hand occurs in the tall red pantry, set diagonally across the room from the refrigerator, which includes a microwave hidden behind a pair of retractable doors. To the right of the pantry, the base freezer is concealed in knotty alder cabinetry. No early 20th-century kitchen would have had an island, so the homeowners found a robust table topped with a 4-inch-thick slab of polished Carrera marble.

"The legs at the bottom of the cabinets are even different," says Smith. "Some have detailing on two sides and others are exposed on three sides." Varying the heights of the pantries and wall cabinets, and including cove moldings on some and not on others, makes the ceiling seem taller than its 8-foot height.

Countertop materials include white-and-gray honed-Calcutta marble and butcher block. "I warned the homeowner that water could damage the butcher block surrounding the farmhouse sink, but she insisted on it and has been vigilant about keeping it oiled," says Smith. "Some time has passed since it was installed and it still looks beautiful."

In a room with so many textures, the floor has to be equally engaging. Smith created a checkerboard pattern by coloring the alternate squares of oak with an ebony stain. Even the Arts and Crafts-style window muntins contribute their part to the retro charm.—*W.J.*

Right: The left-hand wall cabinet includes two small drawers; the right unit has crown molding and antique-look glass in the doors. **Below right:** The middle section of the red-painted pantry houses a microwave behind retractable doors. A small niche for cookbook storage above double ovens mimics the shape of the range arch. **Opposite:** Set on the diagonal like the painted floor design, the marble-topped table is of counter height.

cool ideas!

■ pressed-tin backsplash
■ table-style island
■ mantel over range

company manners

■ As kitchen designer Eric Lieberknecht of Rutt of D.C., in the nation's capitol, will testify, when it comes to creating a great kitchen, new construction is not necessarily a blank slate.

This traditional residence on the Eastern Shore of the Chesapeake Bay is the retirement home of William Kitchel, a former Sub-Zero distributor. The house displays a relaxed elegance throughout, and not surprisingly, Kitchel wanted a timeless design in the kitchen as well. Unfortunately, the space didn't lend itself to a classic kitchen layout.

"The first problem was that there were two big windows on the main wall of the kitchen," Lieberknecht explains. "This seriously cut down the amount of wall space available for cabinetry and appliances."

Another challenge: The kitchen is actually half of a big, open space that includes a cozy keeping room. It functions as an informal eating area, but also has built-in bookshelves, a fireplace, and lounge chairs. "You look directly into the kitchen from the keeping room, so we did not want the kitchen to look too much ... like a kitchen."

How does one design a kitchen that doesn't look like a kitchen? Where does one put such essentials as a refrigerator and a range—especially absent sufficient wall space? Lieberknecht solved these dilemmas by reconceiving the kitchen as an elegantly furnished room.

"The layout challenge drove the decision to locate the refrigerator and freezer in the space between the main working and sitting areas," says Lieberknecht. Once he had decided on the proper placement for the appliances, he disguised them with a traditionally styled custom-made cherry armoire. "I used the Sub-Zero 700 Series because they're the only units you can really disguise well," he explains.

Opposite: Floors of heart-pine, a table-inspired island, built-in bookcases, and crown moldings and other classical architectural details define this keeping-room kitchen. Countertop garages conceal small appliances. **Right:** The Sub-Zero 700 Series tall refrigerator and freezer hide behind the cherry "armoire."

PHOTOGRAPHY: JOHN UMBERGER/REAL IMAGES, INC.

The hard-working kitchen suggests a cozy sitting room.

The professional-style rangetop was positioned between the two windows, a prominent spot, but the only option for placing the exhaust hood. To hide the utilitarian hood in plain sight, Lieberknecht crafted a "mantelpiece." The richly figured cherry suggests fine woodwork and helps bridge the transition between kitchen and keeping room.

To contrast with the stained cherry of the armoire and mantelpiece and to lighten the look, Lieberknecht chose cabinets painted off-white and wiped with a warm brown glaze. The island combines the two finishes with its graceful cherry legs, suggesting a farmhouse table in a former life, over the pale painted finish of the storage unit. Although it holds a sink and pullout garbage bins, the island indeed serves as a farmhouse table, providing an informal dining space.

Lieberknecht chose honed limestone for the island's top, providing textural contrast to the polished granite of the perimeter counters. Although limestone is more susceptible to stains than most other stones, this was not considered a serious drawback because the island is used primarily for eating.

Responding to Kitchel's desire for easy access to cookware, Lieberknecht used only drawers in the lower cabinets. "Wherever possible, I used a drawer instead of a rollout behind a door front," he explains. "With a drawer, it's one step to get to things rather than having to open a door, then pull out a shelf."

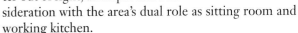

Next to a trio of glass-fronted cabinets, solid-front cabinets provide yet more storage, while three appliance garages help keep clutter out of sight, an important consideration with the area's dual role as sitting room and working kitchen.

"I wanted a kitchen that would be open to the keeping room so that when we entertain, I wouldn't be off in another room by myself," explains Kitchel. "The design is a remarkable success. And functionally, it's a wonderful kitchen. I can get to every inch of storage without straining my back."—*Catherine Censor*

The mantel treatment above the range echoes the fireplace in the adjoining keeping room and is appropriately adorned with a painting and figurines. Behind the rangetop, decorative pressed tin serves as a backsplash. The island counter is made of honed limestone.

fitting furniture

■ Imagine freestanding cabinets that look like fine furniture. Now take the idea to the max. That's how Pittsburgh designer Richard Jacobson of Jacobson/Sylvester Design approached the kitchen renovation of a 1950s-era ranch house. Jacobson partnered up with Thomas D. Trzcinski, CMKBD, of Kitchen & Bath Concepts in Pittsburgh, to open up the kitchen and two small adjoining rooms. The designers wanted to create one large, comfortable room filled with furniture—some of which just happens to house major kitchen appliances.

Jacobson proposed creating workstations with distinct personalities. Thus the rangetop sits in a base of maple stained a deep plum-red that is topped with a backsplash of Brazilian slate, which extends along the entire wall. In contrast, the sink area cabinets are made a lighter, honey-colored pine.

Traditional furniture components link the disparate units, as does the repetitive use of certain materials. Both the rangetop and sink areas have limestone counters; sandblasted stainless steel was used for the farmhouse sink and hood.

The concept was "a little out there," admits Jacobson, but the owners gave it the green light. "I was very taken with the initial design," says one of the homeowners. "The various finishes work well with our antiques and collections."

The room's crowning glory is a transitional piece housing a Sub-Zero Model 700TCI refrigerator-freezer and Model 700TR refrigerator. The panels of the freestanding cherry unit mimic armoire doors and drawers; a pediment tops the unit. Niches house some of the owners' collectibles. The piece could easily be mistaken for an entertainment center. Trzcinski says that the chameleonlike ability of the Sub-Zeros to disappear into any

PHOTOGRAPHY: © 2003 PETER LEACH; STYLING: KATHI KERMES DIXON

design was instrumental to the room's successful design.

Jacobson agrees, "There is no other model on the market that allows this level of customization." The armoire's slightly craftsman, slightly classical details can't quite be pigeonholed, which sums up the comfortably casual feel exuded by the kitchen's eclectic arrangement of "furniture."—*Rebecca Winzenreid*

Opposite: Standing sentry where kitchen and family room merge, a piece of pedimented "furniture" houses two Sub-Zero tall 700 Series units. Above: Distressed-pine cabinets run along the sink wall. The tops of the cabinets mark the original ceiling height, which was raised to open up the space. Pine floor planks laid on the diagonal are recycled from a barn. The freestanding rangetop station wears a painted finish. The hood was sandblasted for a soft gleam. Brazilian slate forms the backsplash.

Like chameleons, the Sub-Zeros disappear into any design.

cool ideas!

- antique sliding pantry door
- industrial-style range hood
- commercial rinser
- exterior ventilation motor

a touch of whimsy

■ For three years before they decided to remodel the kitchen of their Bedford, New York, home, Jack and Paula West cooked and entertained in a dark, unremarkable kitchen. It was "a cramped, 1950s raised-ranch special," says Jack. To remedy the situation, this business owner and his schoolteacher wife turned to kitchen designer Carrie Deane Corcoran of Kitchens by Deane, based in New Canaan and Stamford, Connecticut.

Deane Corcoran transformed the original 180-square-foot kitchen into a 420-square-foot cook's paradise by annexing a former greenhouse. The new work space features an impressive array of professional-grade appliances and a separate "summer kitchen" built two steps down from the main kitchen. "We have seven kids and all are fearless in the kitchen," says Jack. "Now there's enough room for nine of us to cook! We can all work in the kitchen without rubbing elbows."

"The Wests' old kitchen was closed off from the rest of the living areas," says Deane Corcoran. Her directive was to open up the space to make a more gracious and comfortable kitchen where people could gather and enjoy the beautiful

---

Equipped to satisfy a family of serious cooks, this kitchen nonetheless exudes wit and warmth, from its honey-toned cabinetry and the giant poster extolling olive oil to the funky pendant lights that sit over a softly curved eating bar topped with distressed pine.

Like their parents, all seven children love to cook.

views. The owners also asked for ways to incorporate vintage objects they had collected over the years.

Deane Corcoran had the idea of using a salvaged door to hide the pantry. "It was the swinging screen door on an old country store in Connecticut," says the homeowner. "We'd saved it for years but didn't know what to do with it." Using it as a sliding pantry door created a solution to another problem: When the door covers the pantry, it exposes a message center. "We had to figure out a way that we could get in a pantry and a message center but not clutter up the view," Deane Corcoran explains. The sliding door and pantry/ message center design allows an unobstructed view through the kitchen and out the French doors in back.

To keep the space warm and informal, Deane Corcoran and the Wests chose pine cabinets by Draper/DBS with a light honey finish, dark green granite countertops, and a backsplash made of subway-style tiles with a subtle, crackle glaze. A reproduction of a vintage poster for Italian olive oil adds whimsy and color.

The focal point in the kitchen is an 8-foot-long custom stainless-steel hood. The powerful ventilation unit was needed for the extensive cooktop setup, which includes four high-powered gas burners, a deep fryer, a wok, and a grill. A remote blower located outside on the roof keeps the noise level down. Matching the cooktop's versatility is a 36-inch-wide Sub-Zero Model 650 refrigerator-freezer in stainless steel.

Fulfilling the clients' desire for a separate area in the island to store produce, Deane Corcoran tucked stainless-steel Sub-Zero 700 Series refrigerated drawers between the prep sink and the cooktop. Two large sinks and an industrial rinser, along with two stainless-steel dishwasher drawers, make food prep and cleanup equally efficient. "The most satisfying thing," says the homeowner, "is being able to have guests sit at the counter and to serve them right off the tempura fryer, wok, and grill—Japanese steakhouse style."

The Wests credit the success of their kitchen to Deane's diligence in studying their needs, space, and belongings. "What made a huge difference was the almost pathological thoroughness of Deane Corcoran. She opened every single drawer and cabinet, inventoried everything, and took notes like a trial lawyer. It was unbelievable."—*Lynn Prowitt Smith*

Opposite: In counterpoint to the stainless-steel Sub-Zero Model 650 refrigerator-freezer and 700 Series refrigerator drawers in the island, a vintage screen door that conceals a kitchen message center slides to cover the pantry. **Above:** A wall backing a bathroom allows for shallow shelves to hold a collection of glass canisters evocative of a vintage candy store display.

PHOTOGRAPHY: JOHN UMBERGER / REAL IMAGES, INC.

cool ideas!

- beaded-board detailing
- box-bay window
- *trompe l'oeil* painting
- zoned refrigeration

room ▪ with a
view

▪ It's well-known in decorating circles that introducing something new to a room often reveals major shortcomings in the rest of it. That's what happened in a house in suburban Atlanta. A week after the family's new restaurant-style range was installed, they called back their kitchen planner. This time, they ordered a complete kitchen renovation! "Putting in that stove was like pairing new shoes with an old dress—they just didn't work together," says Steen Clausen, CKD, of CSI Kitchen & Bath Studio.

The first step to redoing the room was enlarging the space by nearly 70 percent, achieved by removing walls to the breakfast nook as well as to a portion of the living room. The resulting new room is about 360 square feet compared with the original 220 feet. It also has much more counter space, thanks to the new cooking island, which also houses a second sink. The additional

The vent in the 54-inch-wide stainless-steel hood over the island required going up and out through the second floor. Beaded board, corbels, and cutouts enliven the cherry cabinets. Bookcases are built into the rear of the island.

"We want modern appliances, but we don't always want to look at them."

space comes in handy because both husband and wife like to cook.

Because the two use mainly fresh foods, they asked for more refrigerator than freezer space. Three Sub-Zero 700 Series units give them the flexibility they need. A two-drawer freezer unit sits near the microwave. The full-size fridge is strategically placed to the right of the white porcelain farm sink. In the island, an undercounter two-drawer refrigerator is conveniently located near the pro-style range.

Clausen says that the ability to integrate such appliances as the Sub-Zero units and the Gaggenau dishwasher is much appreciated by his clients. "Today's attitude is that these appliances are essential, but we don't always want to look at them."

The style of the kitchen defies categorization, says Clausen. The new appliances and the efficient arrangement of the room are pure 21st-century American, while decorative faux painting and cherry wood cabinets contribute to a romantic old-world feeling. Continuing that theme is a fluted soffit, and most of the glazed cherry kitchen cabinets boast beaded-board detailing. To add visual excitement, the cabinet housing the farm sink is painted black with blue-and-green highlights. The same finish appears on the bookcases built into the back of the island. Flooring consists of 18-inch-square ceramic tiles laid on the diagonal.

The circular *trompe l'oeil* "window" of faux stone that frames a lush painted garden scene is a decorative focal point in the new breakfast area. A second garden mural is visible from the cooking island. Above gold-flecked black

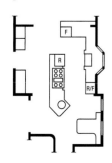

granite counters that extend 6 inches up the wall is a faux-painted stone wall. Decorative painter Bobby Sikes executed the murals and the painted-and-glazed ceiling in similar colors to those used in the rest of the room. Halogen can lights are recessed into the ceiling and the soffit over the main sink.

At the same time they renovated their kitchen, the homeowners also redid their garden, which can be viewed through a new box-bay window. The concurrent improvements nourish both body and soul.—*B.M.*

Opposite: The Sub-Zero 700 Series tall refrigerator sits to the right of the farm sink; coordinated freezer drawers are beside the microwave. The island makes a diagonal jog to house a secondary sink; ceramic floor tiles are laid on the same diagonal. **Above:** Faux-painted stone walls and *trompe l'oeil* landscapes, one in a roundel over the breakfast table, add old world ambience.

PHOTOGRAPHY: JESSIE WALKER; STYLING: AURELIA JOYCE PACE

cool ideas!

- antique range
- reglazed sink
- period lighting
- tin ceiling

time trip

■ When redoing the kitchen in an old house, many would opt for modernity. But not Tom and Kelli Kline, who flouted conventional wisdom by renovating the kitchen in their 1887 Victorian home in Oak Park, near Chicago, in true period style.

"Although I wanted it to be functional, my main goal was to make the kitchen as historically accurate as possible" says Kline. To do so, she researched Victorian kitchens and acquired period appliances, hardware, and lighting—even willingly giving up a garbage disposal unit when the antique sink that she purchased would not accommodate it.

Although the kitchen's wood doors and some moldings were intact, previous owners had ripped out the original cabinets and fixtures. Luckily, neighboring homes still retained identical cabinets, which could be used as a template, and when layers of flooring and wallcovering were stripped, evidence of how the room once had been arranged revealed itself.

By the time she hired kitchen designer Jean Stoffer of River Forest, Illinois, Kline had located an imposing coal-and-gas stove made in 1916, which was already being converted to modern gas. She also had found an antique sink that was being reglazed and a reproduction tin ceiling.

For her part, Stoffer provided the professional expertise to integrate period and modern appliances and custom reproduction cabinetry into a kitchen that boasts 21st-century efficiency. With

Left: The reconditioned 1916 Glenwood Gold Medal stove and a period white-enameled sink with integrated drainboard set the tone of authenticity in this brand new kitchen.
Right: Homeowner Kelli Kline (left) chats with designer Jean Stoffer.

The owner and her friends sit around the kitchen table, knitting and drinking tea.

five doors in the 14-by-18-foot room, each leading to a different part of the house and limiting space for counters and cabinets, functionality was a challenge.

A Sub-Zero Model 650 refrigerator-freezer solved the puzzle of how to get a contemporary unit into the mix. Its overlay panel design permits the use of virtually any facing. In this instance, wood paneling re-creates the look of an old-fashioned icebox, complete with antique hinges and pulls.

Who could imagine a modern kitchen without a dishwasher? Not the Klines. Period authenticity does have its limits! But in keeping with the room's old-time ambience, the dishwasher hides behind an integrated wood panel.

A testament to the success of the renovation is that "most people refuse to believe the cabinets are new," Kline marvels. Made of fir to match the existing woodwork, cabinets wear three coats of shellac—a period finish that imparts a golden glow. Refinished period hardware and both period and reproduction lighting enhance the authenticity.

The elaborately patterned tin ceiling—painted green at cornice level, terra-cotta just above the cornice, and then olive-green, and cream—establishes the color scheme. Walls wear wainscoting to match the cabinets, topped with classic white "subway" tile, and finally, reproduction period wallpaper. The trilevel treatment also helps make the tall room seem cozier. Countertops are honed Carrara marble. Flooring in the work area consists of 1-inch white mosaic tiles with green-and-yellow insets, while the old-fashioned kitchen table—no island here—stands on a wood floor.

"I always like to bring in an antique piece or two into a kitchen, but I had never copied a period so totally until I worked on this one," Stoffer observes. Part of the kitchen's charm undoubtedly derives from a display of antique items, including crockery and utensils from the 19th and early 20th centuries.

"If we had a huge family, perhaps it would not work, but for our lifestyle this kitchen came out great," says Kline. "People say it reminds them of their grandmother's place. My knitting group comes every other Tuesday night and we all sit around the kitchen table, knitting and drinking tea." Were it not for the Sub-Zero and the dishwasher, it could be 1903 instead of a century later.—*Barbara Mayer*

Opposite: The Sub-Zero Model 650 refrigerator-freezer poses as a vintage icebox. To the right of the fridge, the dishwasher is clad to match. **Above:** The warm glow of fir cabinets derives from several coats of shellac. The glass panes of the pantry doors are from the 1880s. **Right:** Enhancing a collection of antique utensils and pottery is wallpaper that reproduces a circa-1880s pattern.

cool ideas!

- mix of floor tiles
- three kinds of cabinet pulls
- antique icebox for storage
- multiple skylights

artist's
palette

■ Who says that owning a vintage house means you must live in a time warp? Not these homeowners: They gutted a dark kitchen in a circa-1830 house in Ipswich, Massachusetts, to arrive at this colorful, light-filled charmer. During the day, the kitchen is flooded with light from four new skylights, several picture windows, and a pair of French doors. At night, a multifaceted lighting system takes over.

Rich hues of turquoise, two yellows, and persimmon add their own brightness on cabinetry, walls, and trim. These colors harmonize beautifully with Brazilian granite counters and the mix of cabinet woods. Wide board pine floors surrounding the tile floor add patina.

The project required considerable construction, including an 8-foot-deep addition and raising the roof to expose the old beams. The kitchen and adjoining dining room together now occupy about 600 square feet.

The homeowners collaborated closely with architect Clifford Boehmer, of Mostue & Associates. "To my mind, what's most interesting about this kitchen is the level of client involvement—especially on the part of the wife,"

Four skylights bathe this colorful kitchen in light. Made by a boatbuilder, the cabinets mix maple, cherry, oak, and walnut. On the floor, pine planks frame a tile runner.

"The clients, especially the wife—a ceramic
artist—were very involved in the design."

says Boehmer. She is a studio potter who also teaches and runs a gallery on the property. Her husband, a structural engineer, specializes in historic reconstruction. Both work a stone's throw from their new kitchen in a remodeled barn.

Not only did the wife supply many of the ideas for the space, she also designed and made the glazed tiles that lend distinction to the quarry tile floor.

An antique oak icebox now serves as a storage piece. A collection of handmade drawer pulls she assembled over the years—and across the country—graces the cabinets: Ceramic knobs distinguish the sink area, green glass knobs appear on a glass-sided cabinet used to display fancy glassware, and hand-cast wrought-iron pulls are used elsewhere in the kitchen.

As Boehmer recalls it, his clients came to him with two requirements. They wanted a kitchen with contemporary function, but not an antiseptic lineup of cabinets. They also preferred individual pieces of furniture to a built-in look. A Model 650 Sub-Zero refrigerator-freezer fits nicely into the format.

"We like the fact that it is only 2 feet deep, and we like the durability of the stainless-steel front," says the architect. The shallow depth means that "things don't get stuck in the back where you can't see them," adds the wife. She also greatly prefers the configuration of refrigerator on top and freezer at bottom.

To contribute to the feeling of a room that was furnished over time, a variety of woods have been employed. A craftsman who usually builds boats made the cabinets. "We used maple, oak, cherry, and walnut, as well as painted finishes such as the turquoise-color pantry and the painted drawer fronts on some cabinets," Boehmer says.

When it comes to lighting a kitchen, he continues, "My rule of thumb is to build in a huge amount of flexibility so you can change the mood of the room." Downlights appear both as standard incandescent fixtures and as small halogens. Four decorative sconces provide uplighting. All lighting is set on dimmers for maximum flexibility. Brightly lit or atmospherically dim, this kitchen has fulfilled its owners' desire for a well-functioning room with a leavening of whimsy and artistry.—*B.M.*

Left: Brazilian granite counters and the stainless-steel door of the Sub-Zero contribute other colors and textures to this eclectic kitchen. **Top Right:** The brilliant color scheme includes a turquoise-painted pantry that suggests freestanding furniture. A layer of granite is sandwiched between the glass-sided display piece and the drawers below. **Right:** The homeowner made the glazed tiles and oversaw their placement in a field of quarry tile.

little red

PHOTOGRAPHY: © KEITH SCOTT MORTON; STYLING: TISHA LEUNG

cool ideas!

- glass-fronted bins
- beaded-board wainscoting
- wooden plate rack
- hinged lift-up window

Opposite: The 30-inch width of the Sub-Zero Model 611 refrigerator-freezer is ideal for this compact kitchen. Tiles on the backsplash depict wine labels. **Left:** Red knobs on the Wolf range add more bright color to this renovated 1870 Connecticut farmhouse kitchen. Shaker-style cabinets with glass-fronted bins hold food staples.

■ A hodgepodge of outmoded appliances and Victorian windows lined this 110-square-foot kitchen when the owners, a Connecticut engineer and his wife, bought the house. The couple loved the 1870 house's quaint appeal but had to decide whether a kitchen addition made more sense than renovating the existing space to get everything they needed for 21st-century living.

"Beth Veillette was the only designer we talked to who understood our home's antique personality and who didn't want to change its footprint by building a kitchen off the rear of the house," says the husband. He'd contacted Veillette, of Hanford Cabinet & Woodworking in Old Saybrook, Connecticut, after seeing a renovated kitchen she designed that was featured in a kitchen-design magazine.

Veillette's solution was to commandeer 40 square feet from an adjacent powder room to enlarge the kitchen without actually adding on. She then reconfigured the space by moving some preexisting kitchen doors and changing the size of one window. "Taking the back door 3 feet away from the corner allowed a long stretch of counter to extend from the cottage-style sink the couple wanted," Veillette explains.

"The husband was restoring all the windows in the house, and he shortened one overlooking their beautiful backyard pond so the sink could fit underneath," she continues. The window was adapted to open from the bottom and makes the view of the pond 20 feet away the visual heart of the kitchen. Veillette then placed the refrigerator and range against the opposite wall within easy access of the sink.

The owners knew they wanted a Wolf range and Sub-Zero refrigerator. Both appliances are right at home in the barn-red period look the couple requested to assert the house's vintage character. "I love the range's red knobs in the red kitchen," says the wife, "and the way stainless steel gives the kitchen

Respecting the character and history of the house was a given.

a professional-looking edge." The Sub-Zero Model 611 refrigerator-freezer is narrow enough to make way for a wide period-style mantel hood over the range along the same wall.

Flat-paneled Shaker-style cabinetry over the Sub-Zero's door and freezer drawer camouflage the modern appliance. A microwave oven is cleverly hidden too, behind a retractable cupboard panel at the end of the L-shaped countertop. Glass-fronted drawers on either side of the range are styled like bins to hold food staples. Additional storage backs up to the glass-fronted slots.

The wormy-chestnut countertop is salvaged from 100-year-old New England barn siding. Chestnut flooring replaces the pine subfloor, which turned out to be too damaged to restore. "The warmth of wood is wonderful with the red-painted cabinets, and it's a real complement to the utilitarian black-and-white Luna Pearl granite on work surfaces around much of the kitchen," Veillette says. The granite extends beyond the sink to a window-front desk, where the owners can pay bills while observing the waterfowl on the pond.

A time-honored way of storing items, pegs crown the beaded-board wainscoting that wraps around the kitchen. Most of the furnishings, if not antique, look as if they had been accrued over the kitchen's long history. Veillette set the stage by adding the freestanding plate rack. "I wanted it to look old, as if the owners found an antique for the spot," she says. The couple subsequently bought the Victorian kitchen table, hooked rug, and 19th-century oiled-bronze pendant light fixture.

"Grandma's kitchen with a kick" is how the couple describes the renovation that spared them an expensive addition and honors the spirit of the house.—*Susan Stiles Dowell*

Opposite: Relocating the back door from the corner made it possible to run the granite counter the length of the sink wall. **Right, from top:** An antique-style plate rack complements the chestnut floor and counter. A window was refitted and hinged at the top for an old-fashioned look. Luna Pearl granite extends to the desk.

cool ideas!

- denim-blue cabinets
- stucco range hood
- step stool in toe-kick
- quartz-composite counters

mood
indigo

With its hand-distressed blue cabinets and delicate, hand-painted tiles, the kitchen of this Los Angeles-area home is prettiness personified. But looks can be deceiving: The room is designed to meet the rigorous demands of a serious cook. Homeowner Laura Davis prepares daily meals for herself and husband Roger, as well as a weekly dinner for their extended family. And that's when she's not busy creating gourmet treats from the fruit and herbs she grows in her garden. Among her specialties are strawberry jam, grapefruit marmalade, herb vinegars and oils, and even house-cured olives. "The kitchen is the perfect space to work in," she declares.

But the kitchen wasn't always such a joy. In the early 1980s the couple had done a basic renovation, which was in keeping with the house's English-cottage style. But the rustic decor now seemed rather dark; nor had the remod-

Right: Recessed-panel cabinets were stained denim-blue, then hand-distressed, before receiving a catalyzed protective finish. The simple recessed-panel doors are repeated on the door panels of the Sub-Zero Model 690 refrigerator-freezer. **Left:** Laura and Roger Davis bring a bit of their garden's bounty into the kitchen.

PHOTOGRAPHY: MICHAEL GARLAND. STYLING: SUNDAY HENDRICKSON

The island has become the kitchen's social center.

eling addressed the kitchen's major drawbacks: inadequate storage space and an oppressively low ceiling.

This time around, the Davises wanted a lighter, sunnier kitchen where guests could enjoy informal meals. "I knew exactly what I wanted," Laura says. Her priorities: an island, "miles of countertops," and storage space galore.

For the preliminary design and decor, the homeowners turned to Los Angeles interior designer Dan Zimmerman, with whom they have had a long relationship. Kitchen designer Geoffrey Frost, of Downsview Kitchens, also in Los Angeles, was called in to assist with the layout and selection of cabinets.

To gain much-needed headroom, the pair reclaimed what was formerly attic space. In its place is a new vaulted ceiling with beams that hide recessed lighting. To further open up the room and take advantage of garden views, the designers had tall windows installed in the breakfast area. Finally, they pushed back a wall separating the kitchen from a service hall to create space for a new cooking and baking center. The kitchen now measures about 20 by 25 feet.

"Raising the ceiling really increased the volume of space in the room," says Frost. "It now feels twice as big, even though

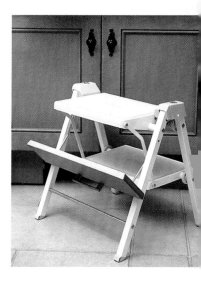

we probably actually added only about 4 more feet." The new layout saves steps because everything is close at hand. "The prep sink is a real step saver because Laura doesn't have to keep moving back to the sink wall when she is working at the island," Frost adds.

The island includes the deep farmhouse sink that Laura had been craving, both for its homey style and its capacity to handle large stock pots. The island also addresses storage needs with an abundance of specialized drawers and cabinets, along with a

Left: Hand-painted tiles edge the stucco hood and continue along the tumbled marble backsplash, accenting the cabinet color. This area was once a service porch. The Sub-Zero Model 424 wine storage unit sits below a quartz-composite counter.
Above: A step stool pulls out from the toe-kick below the main sink.

The garden's grapefruit
and olive trees and
strawberry plants yield
gourmet treats.

Sub-Zero Model 700BR refrigerator and Model 424 wine storage unit. Guests now gravitate to the island as Roger serves wine and appetizers, while Laura puts the finishing touches on a meal.

And how does the cook feel about being at the hub of the action? "I like to have people hang out at the island," says Laura. "I used to feel so isolated in the kitchen—there was no room for anyone else."

Also handy for entertaining—and one of Roger's few demands for the new kitchen—is a refrigerator that dispenses ice and water. This desire was fulfilled by the selection of a Sub-Zero Model 690 side-by-side refrigerator-freezer. Its custom panels blend in with the rest of the blue cabinetry.

Precisely because she spends so much time cooking and cleaning up, Laura took the attitude of a professional chef when it came to finishes and materials. "She wanted everything to be low maintenance, without a lot of fuss and bother," recalls Frost. Consequently, counters are a quartz composite, selected for its durability and stain resistance, rather than more porous granite. Porcelain floor tiles mimic

limestone, but don't need to be sealed as the stone would require. Even the cabinetry was chosen with an eye toward practicality: Its catalyzed finish is stain- and acid-resistant.

The homeowners describe the color of the cabinets as "stonewashed French denim." A color stain and hand distressing allow the warmth of the wood to shine through. The Davises knew from the start that they wanted cabinets reminiscent of the color of the Aegean Sea. "Blue is so calming," explains Laura, "and it works with the blue sky that we always have here in California."

Another perk: Roger, who is red-green color blind, can perceive blue tones, which allows him to enjoy the kitchen as much as his wife clearly does.—*Rebecca Winzenreid*

Opposite: The eating area overlooks extensive gardens through a full-length fixed window. **Above left:** An appliance garage and a television cabinet bridge the area between the rangetop and the desk. **Above right:** A butcher-block counter frames the apron-front sink in the island, which includes such customized interior fittings as a knife block, a mixer lift, and pull-out pantries.

old-world
kitchens

■ Imagine a world of simplicity and elegance, where a hint of European antiquity lends a feeling of genteel stability. That's the old-world style you'll encounter in this section. Whether you prefer the ambiance of a Tuscan villa or a kitchen that pays homage to the Italian Renaissance, you are sure to find myriad ideas on the following pages. Skilled designers used distressed paint finishes, tiled range hoods, and terra-cotta floors to echo centuries past in these kitchens—but consider gently vaulted alcoves, stone counters, or well-worn tapestry rugs to evoke the soothing style of old-world charm to welcome friends and family into your kitchen.

The French provincial-style range hood is the focal point in this kitchen, supported by corbels and hand-painted flowers. Cabinets wear a mixture of glazed and stained finishes, a hallmark of old-world style.

DESIGNERS: MICHAEL AND LYNNE MERCATANTE; PHOTOGRAPHY: © PETER LEACH

cool ideas!

- tiled range hood
- open display shelves
- "picnic table" dining area
- distressed paint finishes

villa revisited

■ Real estate professionals will tell you it's the kitchen that often sells the house. That's exactly what this luxurious yet informal kitchen with an Italian country feeling was designed to do. It is the centerpiece of a new "Tuscan villa" style house in Portland, Oregon, which was part of a tour known as the "Street of Dreams." The kitchen did its job: The house sold well before the show ended.

According to designer Charles Buller, president of Park Place Wood Products, the builder asked for "an American version of the perfect Italian country kitchen." Buller designed and installed the 380-square-foot kitchen, which is part of a multipurpose space that also includes the family room.

Flooring zones the two rooms—tile in the kitchen and wood in the family room—as does a large buffet located at the edge of the tile floor.

The result is romantic and charming but lacks none of the latest technology-driven bells and whistles. Appliances such as the 48-inch Sub-Zero Model 632 refrigerator-freezer satisfy the builder's demand for the best of every-

Left: Glass-fronted upper cabinets and open shelves contribute to a spacious feeling. The range hood and wall behind the stove are covered with Malibu tiles. The change in flooring from terra-cotta tile to jarrah wood signals the transition from kitchen to family room. **Right:** The "picnic table" on an X base embraces the island.

thing. And the choice of materials and numerous decorative flourishes raise the charm quotient well above the bar.

The fridge shares a wall with a small pantry with pull-out shelves. Using the same wood fronts integrates the two units, creating the illusion of a single, generous pantry. A center island accommodates a dishwasher and a second sink, storage drawers, and a place for informal dining.

Natural and handcrafted materials include countertops of honed granite, terra-cotta tile floors, and colorful glazed tiles that enliven the range hood and wall behind the range. Full of character and warmth, wood is used throughout the room in cabinets, ceiling beams, and decorative details.

Two fat corbels appear to support the tiled range hood; scalloped edgings ornament some cabinets. For added richness, Buller used two woods for cabinets and trim: rough-textured white oak and smooth jarrah wood. The contrasts in texture enhance the handcrafted effect.

Although not well-known in the United States, jarrah wood is gaining a foothold. Native to Australia, it is a hardwood that is termite resistant and in its natural state comes in a fairly wide range of hues, including what might be mistaken for mahogany.

Buller likes the color variations as well as the fact that the wood is easy to work with and used it throughout the room, including the family room floor. The buffet that zones the kitchen from the family room is made of jarrah. So is the "picnic table" on an X base that surrounds the island.

Upper cabinets have doors with glass inserts. They and the open shelves that distinguish the corner near the

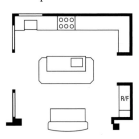

microwave have been layered with several shades of paint, then ragged and distressed to create a rich deep color. The porcelain farm sink sits in a handcrafted oak cabinet.

If decorative details suggest the past, lighting is completely up-to-date with multiple types for flexibility. Recessed halogen ceiling lights handle general illumination, while low-voltage undercabinet strips illuminate work surfaces.

For atmosphere, concealed low-voltage incandescent strips create a pool of light at ceiling level and light glass-fronted cabinet interiors. Three decorative fixtures with handblown glass shades light the island.

"You would probably never find a kitchen like this in Tuscany," admits Buller. "This is an Americanized version of a Tuscan kitchen, which gives you the advantage of top appliances and artistry, all in one entity."—*B.M.*

Top: The Sub-Zero Model 632 side-by-side refrigerator-freezer is integrated into the cabinetry with doors of jarrah wood banded by stained oak. The same mix appears in the island-buffet. **Above:**

Twisted wrought-iron drawer pulls and a towel bar are finished to suggest age. **Right:** Beneath the range hood, a fancifully carved wood corbel (one of a pair) is purely decorative.

cool ideas!

■ corbeled range hood
■ decorative arches
■ slate floor
■ narrow wine rack

italian renaissance

■ Located near downtown Minneapolis, the city's revitalized Warehouse District includes an eclectic mix of renovated lofts carved out of former factories, as well as new developments. It was here that a couple of empty nesters chose a new villalike condo, strategically sited beside the Mississippi River.

Although the actual living space of their new residence was large, light, and airy, the kitchen was typically undersized with approximately 150 square feet of space. This did not suit the homeowners, who enjoy cooking and frequently host parties, both for business and pleasure. They turned to kitchen designer Tricia Hauser Tidemann, of North Star Kitchens in Minneapolis, to achieve their desire for a functional but warm Tuscan-style kitchen.

The first challenge Tidemann faced was to reconcile the couple's wish list with the reality of the space. "There were only 15 lineal feet of contiguous wall space for the kitchen," recalls Tidemann. "And they wanted a 5-foot-wide AGA range!" Tidemann convinced the homeowners to go with a more modest two-oven AGA, at 39½ inches wide, which was more than adequate for their needs. "This allowed for more usable storage and prep space on both sides of the range," says the designer.

To make the kitchen as efficient as it was aesthetically pleasing, Tidemann combined open storage for decorative and often-used items with well-placed drawers to hold baking supplies, cutlery, cookware, and linens. "Building in refrigeration also helped keep the look uniform and didn't break up the line of vision," she observes.

To maximize refrigeration space, the designer installed the Sub-Zero integrated 700 Series. The primary unit, a 27-inch-wide Model 700TCI refrigerator-freezer, sits neatly in its own niche with room to spare for a neighboring bake center. Model 700BR refrigerated drawers, positioned to the right of the range, within easy reach of the sink, add supplementary storage and facilitate meal preparation.

In keeping with the home's architecture, Tidemann took an elegant Tuscan approach, more akin to a Florentine palazzo than a country farmhouse. Within gently vaulted alcoves, maple cabinets provide such old-world details as a slightly distressed, aged finish and handsome moldings. Counters and backsplash are sumptuously veined marble. The floor is a utilitarian but lush black slate.

"The island, too, was designed to be functional and to look like a beautiful piece of furniture," says Tidemann, pointing out its finely turned legs and matching cabinetry base. The room's focal point, however, is the stately custom range hood, designed and fabricated by a local contractor. It is the ultimate complement to the classical sense of proportion and balance evidenced in this kitchen.—*Linda C. Lentz*

Polished marble counters and a black slate floor establish the elegant ambience in this Tuscan-style kitchen. The Sub-Zero Model 700TCI refrigerator-freezer is integrated into the cabinetry in a niche that also contains open storage. Model 700BR refrigerator drawers sit to the right of the range. The capacious island is fitted with an apron-front sink and a dishwasher.

cool ideas!

- scenic backsplash
- reclaimed chestnut floor
- decorative stonework
- honed-granite counters

scaling ▪ new
heights

■ Can a newly constructed "spec" home convey warmth, charm, and even soul? With carefully selected materials and proper planning, kitchen designer Chris L. Haight and architect Ken Pieper say it can.

Witness his dramatic tribute to the Steamboat Springs, Colorado, setting of this new house. The spirited design is proof positive that the past doesn't have a monopoly on architectural romance.

The builder of this large ranch home was emphatic that the kitchen should be its showplace. While most kitchen designers draw on existing architectural elements for inspiration, Haight was asked to lead the way. The builder was willing to have the materials and design themes established in the kitchen dictate the rest of the house's decorative details.

Light and space were already abundant. The kitchen measures 21 by 16 feet. Add in the adjoining breakfast room, and the area extends a total of 32 feet. Because the adjacent great-room has large window walls, there is plenty of ambient light. Sunlight also streams in the kitchen's own picture window, which frames a heart-stopping view of the mountains.

Haight selected materials that referred to the natural world: Locally quarried and dry-stacked stone frames the built-in grill, imbuing the otherwise traditional kitchen with a craggy, rustic feel. This initial impression is reinforced with pine

The rough textures of pine cabinets, dry-stacked stone (housing the grill), and recycled chestnut floors give this brand-new kitchen a warm, lived-in feel. The honed-granite counter in the main work area is distinguished by an ogee edge.

"The kitchen fits the rustic, Western design spirit of Steamboat Springs."

cabinets and flooring made of wormy-chestnut planks reclaimed from old beams. To avoid the cold look of metal or porcelain, knobs are also pine.

On the island, built of cherry, robust corner posts suggest the legs of a sturdy antique farm table. The honed Juperana Classico Rio granite used for all the counter-tops adds more rough-hewn texture. (Polished granite would have appeared too contemporary.)

Haight worked with the builder's finish carpenters to make sure the cherry stairway, visible from the kitchen, was in keeping with the color and design of the island. The breakfast area's built-in china cabinet is also crafted of cherry. Its glass panels are repeated above the lintel on the kitchen's stone wall.

Molding and window trim throughout the house match the pine kitchen cabinets. But without a doubt, the kitchen's most unusual touch is the granite backsplash carved to replicate the mountain range visible beyond the window.

For all its rustic good looks, the kitchen is also a comfortable space in which to work. The barbecue grill vents to the outdoors. Double ovens are placed out of the main work area, to the right of the stone wall, with a nearby warming drawer.

The cooktop is centrally located in the island, along with one dishwasher and a prep sink. (A second dishwasher hides behind paneling to the left of the main sink.) The Sub-Zero side-by-side Model 690 to the right of the sinks is convenient to the breakfast room. Cutlery dividers, hidden spice racks, and a lazy Susan provide organized storage.

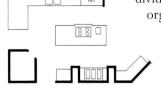

The end result of Haight's careful design is a kitchen that reflects a tangible sense of place. Like the Rocky Mountains, it speaks of grandeur, integrity, and permanence.—*C.C.*

Opposite: The kitchen overlooks the Rocky Mountains, which are rendered in granite relief along the backsplash. The dishwasher to the left of the sink masquerades as a set of drawers. **Above:** For living room looks, the Sub-Zero Model 690 refrigerator-freezer and most other appliances are paneled to match the pine cabinets.

cool ideas!

- tiles laid diagonally
- see-through cabinets
- copper range hood

a new
angle

■ Remaking a long narrow room with a surfeit of doors but a deficiency of windows brought out the talents of kitchen designers Matthew Quinn and Beth Barfield of Design Galleria, in Atlanta. The clients, a busy couple in their thirties who work in banking and real estate, wanted a glamorous kitchen with a multitude of appliances, and plenty of both natural light and storage space.

"The only way that we could give them everything they wanted was by designing two pairs of glass-backed upper cabinets and placing them over two new windows," says Quinn. The tricky installation required precision in measuring and fitting the cabinets. This stratagem to simultaneously gain light and storage space also offers a decorative payoff: When the sun shines in, the glassware and dishes stored in the cabinets sparkle; at night, lights mounted inside the cabinets achieve a similar magical effect.

The two unusual cabinets flank an equally unique oversize rangetop hood, covered in squares of acid-aged copper tacked down with copper nails. A clear epoxy finish helps keep it tarnish free. Alderwood cabinets beneath the

Glass-fronted cabinets installed directly in front of windows flank a copper rangetop hood made with overlapping sheets of metal. The floor's diagonal pattern marries foot-square travertine tiles and walnut planks. The double doors of the Sub-Zero Model 632 refrigerator-freezer are a boon in the narrow kitchen.

The refrigerator's double doors make it ideal for the relatively narrow space.

Opposite: A counter of Verde Butterfly granite surrounds an undermount stainless-steel sink on the island; a secondary, apron-front sink on the far wall is made of soapstone. **Right top:** File drawers below and tall cabinets above the desk handle clutter. **Right bottom:** Beneath the copper-topped section of the island, Sub-Zero Model 700BR refrigerator drawers hold soft drinks while the Model 424 wine storage unit keeps bottles of red and white at correct temperatures.

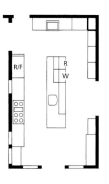

48-inch-wide rangetop hold pots and pans in deep drawers. Extrawide, shallow drawers hold an array of utensils and pullout cabinets on either side of the rangetop accommodate spices and condiments.

A 48-inch-wide Sub-Zero side-by-side refrigerator-freezer anchors one end of this hardworking wall. "The 24-inch depth and its double doors make it ideal for the relatively narrow space," says Quinn. Although the room is a generous 25 feet long, it is just under 14½ feet wide.

Forming a compact work triangle, the main sink is located in a multifunction, multilevel island. The island's food preparation area is topped with Verde Butterfly granite, as is an overhang for informal dining. A raised portion that functions as a bar is clad in acid-washed copper to match the range hood.

Fronting the bar area is both a Sub-Zero Model 700BR refrigerator and a Model 424 wine storage unit. When the couple entertains, guests congregate around the bar, well out of the way of the main food preparation area on the other side of the island.

A long line of floor-to-ceiling wall cabinets directly behind the island provides ample pantry space, while using only 14 precious inches of depth. One pantry stores food staples, another such small appliances as a toaster, coffeemaker, and microwave oven, keeping them handy without cluttering up the counters.

To visually expand the narrow space, Quinn and Barfield designed a travertine-tile and walnut-plank floor, laid on the diagonal. The tile backsplash behind the rangetop reprises the diagonal theme; a decorative inset beneath the range hood echoes its curved frame.

In keeping with the verdant views outside, the room's color scheme is based on nature's palette. Perimeter cabinets wear an antiqued beige finish called "Buckskin," the island cabinets a soft olive-green-painted finish. Decorative touches include an elaborate crown molding in keeping with the style of the house, which is a brick Georgian.

The owners aren't the only ones who love the new kitchen. Their Labrador retrievers, one black and one yellow, have taken to sitting for hours at a time on the low storage bench in front of an over-size window to the left of the cooking-area window. Sounds like the two big design challenges were met to their satisfaction as well!—*Barbara Mayer*

vintage
simplicity

In remodeling a guest house in Bernardsville, New Jersey, a couple wanted the kitchen to have a rustic look without sacrificing function. Working with Nadia R. Jaworskyj, of Nadia's Theme Creative Interior Designs, Jeffrey Kennedy, CKD, of J Kennedy Design, created a U-shaped facility that exudes timeless charm.

"Our clients wanted cabinets that looked handmade," Kennedy recalls. So the designers encased the refrigerator-freezer and the fronts of the upper cabinets in knotty pine beaded board, then stained it. Poplar base cabinets are painted teal blue with a red undercoat. "We distressed the finish to look as though red cabinets had once been blue, but the over-paint had started to crack," he says.

The effect convincingly simulates the age of many of the antiques in the

Faux-painted walls and stained beams enhance the vintage look of the 9-by-11½-foot kitchen. The Sub-Zero Model 700 TCI refrigerator with two freezer drawers hides behind custom doors with strap hardware.

guest house. The vintage feeling extends to other elements: The new copper sink with an apron front was distressed and antiqued and the bronze faucet oil-rubbed for the look of age. Counters are maple butcher block with a backsplash of tumbled marble tiles.

"We chose a Sub-Zero 700 Series refrigerator-freezer because we could make it resemble a tall pantry," Ken-nedy explains. "It is concealed behind scrubbed pine beaded board, complete with vintage-style wrought-iron handles and mock strap hinges."

The new Elmira Stove Works range re-creates a century-old design, but functions in a contemporary manner with gas burners and an electric oven. "And when you lift up the front of the ducting hood, there is a glass panel with digital controls," adds Kennedy. "So there is a real contrast between the way the appliance looks and how it functions." The same might be said of this compact kitchen.—*M.K.*

PHOTOGRAPHY: RICHARD SEXTON

hidden
assets

■ When architect-builder Stephen Chauvin, AIA, and his wife, whose three sons have now left the nest, decided to renovate their 1,400-square-foot cottage a stone's throw from New Orleans, they gutted it right down to its heart-pine floors. The greatest change to the 1920s bungalow-style house was in the kitchen. Here, the couple removed walls and windows and enclosed a 9-foot-deep porch, which also gained a vaulted ceiling.

The remodeled kitchen is an intriguing mix of sophistication and whimsy, where pared-down efficiency is deftly combined with ornate elements. For starters, a pair of gilded-and-carved angels stands guard on either side of an enameled LaCanache range, which Chauvin describes as "like a piece of jewelry."

Representing the practical component is a pot-filler spigot above the range. It is mounted on Absolute Black granite, the same mate-

Left: This highly personal space designed for an avid cook contains no upper cabinetry. Appliances are tucked behind architectural elements. **Right:** A salvaged door opens the kitchen to breezes and a view of the yard and pool.

rial selected for the flanking countertops. Over the large range, two ventilation systems share a sweeping stainless-steel hood.

To the right of the range, in the area that was once the porch, a pair of 18th-century French parlor doors conceals a Sub-Zero 700 Series refrigerator and freezer. "The doors were purchased by a client who ultimately decided not to use them," recalls Chauvin. "They were a perfect fit for the Sub-Zero units. It's important to make a room an extension of an owner's wishes. Because the 400 and 700 Series can be fully integrated into cabinetry, I can put on antique doors, contemporary ones, or anything else to create the appropriate environment."

Between the refrigerator and freezer, Chauvin installed a simple low black cabinet and mirrored the wall between the elaborate antique doors. "My wife likes to bake, so I created a cabinet with a mixer in it that can easily be taken out," he explains.

In the island are a dishwasher and a pair of stainless-steel sinks set in the counter of Emerald Pearl granite. A raised bar, which serves for informal meals, is constructed from a single piece of Spanish cedar that has been ebonized, then finished in urethane. Robust curvaceous cast-iron brackets support the bar counter.

Most of the wood cabinetry is painted pale blue, but unlike the walls of a similar hue, an amber glaze gives it an antiqued finish. In another Baroque flourish, the ceiling is painted silver.

Where there was once a window, Chauvin installed a double exterior door he found in a salvage shop. He added glass shutters and a pediment to admit light and breezes. To the right of the door, floor-to-ceiling cabinets are surfaced in textured glass applied over mirror, which gives the illusion that they are lit from within.

Behind the center doors, a bar unit and small sink, conveniently located out of the kitchen's main traffic flow, share space with a gilded 19th-century Spanish tabernacle. A steam oven, icemaker, and Sub-Zero Model 427R wine storage unit that incorporates two refrigerated drawers have also found a home here.

Across from the island, a paneled vestibule whose doors fold back into the paneling leads to the den. When the doors are shut, the den can double as a guest room. The paneling turns the corner into one wall of the kitchen to include hidden storage for a microwave oven and accoutrements for making coffee.

Other one-of-a-kind details are old hardware pulls in the shape of angels and sunbursts and a narrow storage cabinet concealed in the paneling beyond the stove. To the left of the stove (not shown) are a television and stereo, another cabinet for plates, and a walk-in pantry that includes a water dispenser and a telephone.

Chauvin and his wife love their finished results: "It's a comfortable room, one that's the perfect size for the two of us," he concludes.—*Kathleen Mahoney*

Open-and-shut cases:
Opposite: A paneled passageway with hinged-foldout doors leads to the den. The coffee station is to the left. **Near right:** The floor-to-ceiling unit features textured-glass fronts installed over mirror that conceal a bar and a Sub-Zero Model 427R wine storage unit. **Far right:** Ornate 18th-century doors cover a Sub-Zero Series 700 refrigerator and freezer. Between them, a cabinet houses a mixer.

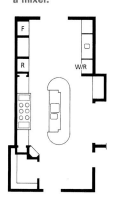

cool ideas!

■ copper range hood
■ leaded-glass cabinet doors
■ honed-slate counters

mountain high

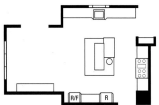

Opposite: Suggesting a large armoire, a pair of Sub-Zero tall 700 Series units flanks a pantry. **Above:** The French-country-style cabinets are enriched with detailing. Leaded-glass fronts on upper units provide a foil to the elaborately carved wood.

■ A brand new French Provincial chateau with dramatic views of the Rocky Mountains patiently awaits an owner. When it came to the design of its spacious kitchen, Aspen Custom Builders turned to kitchen designer Kelly McGuire, of Mountain Valley Cabinetry in Basalt, Colorado.

"No expense was spared. The builder told us to pull out all the stops," McGuire recalls. "Everything we selected is of the highest quality."

In keeping with the style of the house, McGuire glazed and distressed cabinets of knotty alder, raising them off the floor on substantial feet to give the illusion of freestanding furniture. "While it's costly, detailing such as crown moldings, radius end panels, and crown capitals adds richness and dimension," notes McGuire.

Such tasks as cooking, preparation, cleanup, and refrigeration are deliberately zoned. A Sub-Zero tall 700 Series refrigerator and refrigerator-freezer bookend a recessed cabinet with bifold doors that stores a microwave and other small appliances. "I especially like the 700 Series because I can fully integrate the units into cabinetry," says McGuire. "Without grilles, they look like furniture."

Similarly, two dishwasher drawer units flank the main sink. A large professional-style range, set in a niche, is the focal point of the room. Over it, a hand-tooled copper hood with wood corbels and banding relates to the reclaimed timber trusses that support the cathedral ceiling.

In the center of the room, a large island, its countertops covered in blue slate honed to a soft finish, contains a small prep sink, a 9-inch-thick maple butcher block, and two warming drawers. The designer raised the center level to minimize the island's bulk and provide a display area, storage, and electrical access. All this kitchen needs now is an appreciative new owner to bring it to life.—*Kathleen Mahoney*

cool ideas!

- "castle door" treatment
- wrought-iron entry gate
- stone "hearth" over range

cultural
blend

■ When it came to creating her dream kitchen, the sophisticated fashion executive knew exactly what she wanted, explains interior designer Diane Boyer, ASID, of Diane Boyer Interiors, a division of Bill Berhle Associates, in Verona, New Jersey. The homeowner had lived all over the world and had spent a significant amount of time in the Middle East. She specified a design that would blend Spanish, Mediterranean, and Middle Eastern themes.

"My client had seen a picture of a castle that had a huge fireplace with a stove in it," explains Boyer. "We took that idea and used it to create this very interesting

kitchen where the range almost looks like it's set in a baronial fireplace."

To make the client's dream a reality, Boyer and kitchen designer Bob Lidsky of The Hammer and Nail in Wyckoff, New Jersey, had to solve some (literally) big problems. The chosen design elements—stone, dark woods, muted colors, and massive scale—threatened to make the space dark and somber. How could they achieve a lively, vibrant room without sacrificing a substantial, richly textured look? The answer lay in the careful selection of materials that would provide texture and color.

The heart of the kitchen is the stone floor-to-ceiling "hearth" housing the professional-style range. Hand-carved in Mexico, the massive structure required a foundation in the basement. The treatment of the refrigerator and freezer reinforces the old-world look. Sub-Zero 700 Series tall units hide behind panels of solid cherry designed to mimic medieval castle doors. The panels were deliberately

To create the look of a medieval castle, arches, Moroccan lighting fixtures, and salvaged beams complement the treatment of the Sub-Zero refrigerator and freezer doors. Rough-hewn cherry is studded with rusted decorative nails and iron pulls. Cabinets have been distressed to suggest the patina of age. Art glass and pottery—gathered on trips abroad—add warmth and authenticity.

The kitchen gets almost as much use as a commercial space would.

made to look rough to evoke handcrafted authenticity. Rusted-iron decorative nails, known as clavos, and pulls add to the impression of age and patina.

To balance and enliven these elements, most of the cherry cabinets were painted a warm yellow. Lidsky then had areas of the doors sanded to simulate wear before applying a low-luster glaze. Other cabinets were distressed, treated to fake cracks, and given a very dark glaze. Here and there, corners were chiseled down so that the brand-new kitchen looks as if it has been in continual use for generations. "We wanted the cabinets to look worn but not tired," explains Lidsky.

Architectural flourishes reinforce the antique theme. Hand-hewn oak beams, salvaged from a barn, display a deep color and irregular surface that helps to unify the ceiling with the rest of the room. Plaster corbels—which reprise the countertops' supports—arched doorways, and the niche above the refrigerator add pleasing curves and balance the square, heavy pieces found elsewhere. The wrought-iron detailing at the doorways and over the range add a lacy transparency in counterpoint to the stone and dark wood.

The choice of countertops furthers the juggling act. The island features dark slate; other counters are light limestone. Boyer cautions that these materials aren't the right choice for everyone. Slate can scratch and limestone is absorbent. "Our client entertains every weekend," the designer says. "This kitchen is getting almost as much use as a commercial kitchen would. And because limestone can absorb stains, it's getting a little more 'character' than the owner would have liked. She's already had to reseal the countertops twice."

Despite the stains and oil rings, the client revels in her kitchen, which is exactly the personal, unique space she wanted. "This kitchen is rich and exotic, yet highly functional," says Boyer. "Golden and warm, it's a tapestry of color, texture, and wonderful natural materials."—*Catherine Censor*

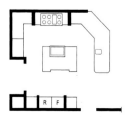

Opposite: Wrought-iron architectural accents and handpainted ceramic tile add drama and a sense of history. The island's slate surface is shaped to accommodate robust corbels. **Above:** The stone "hearth" was carved in Mexico. The range's exhaust fan is hidden behind wrought-iron tracery.

cool ideas!

- limestone walls
- oven in armoire
- double islands
- mosaic backsplash

understated
elegance

■ "As we began planning the project, I recall asking, 'Why shouldn't a kitchen be as beautiful as a piece of quality furniture?'" says Jackie Cottrill of the kitchen in her new Atlanta home. Kitchen designer Shirley McFarlane, CKD, of Kitchensmith, answered, "It can." A building coordinator and interior design consultant, Cottrill wanted state-of-the-art appliances but not a stereotypical appearance. "Of course, the challenge was to make the kitchen both functional and beautiful," McFarlane adds.

The color scheme of a rich honey-brown with black accents evolved from chandeliers Cottrill had designed, as well as from the wood tones of a china cabinet for the dining room. McFarlane chose custom maple cabinets with a multistep stained-and-glazed finish such as those applied to fine furniture.

Stepping out the cabinets along the window wall and adding an apron with decorative cast-iron brackets under the sink help to break up an otherwise long stretch of cabinetry. Details such as turned legs on the two islands and robust 1¼-inch-thick cabinet doors also contribute to the living room manners. Cabinet doors on the islands and a wall unit housing a convection oven and television wear a black baked-enamel finish for contrast.

With furniture-quality doors accented by reeded col-

Left: The kitchen takes its color cues from chandeliers designed by the homeowner that feature high-flying monkeys. The mosaic of granite, travertine, and marble—some polished, some honed—is inset in the limestone backsplash. The ventilation system hides behind a cabinet valance. **Right:** A cast-iron mermaid bracket, one of two, adds decorative flair to the sink apron.

"Why shouldn't a kitchen be as beautiful as a piece of quality furniture?"

umns, a decorative toe-kick and furniture pulls, two Sub-Zero 700 Series refrigerator-freezers blend seamlessly into the room. So seamlessly says Cottrill, that when more than 2,000 people viewed the kitchen during the Junior League of Atlanta Tour of Homes, "everyone asked, 'Where's the fridge?'"

The islands, both topped with Norwegian Brown Magic granite, have unobtrusive undermount black fire-clay sinks fitted with garbage disposals. "My husband and I love to give dinner parties. When we're entertaining, this kitchen works great because there are two work stations," explains Cottrill.

The island closer to the range includes a warming drawer and is used for food prep and unloading groceries. The one closer to the black wall cabinet housing the television is convenient for meals on the run or arranging flowers. It is also handy for guests who want to add finishing touches to a dish they've brought for an informal get-together.

A butler's pantry accommodates china, glassware, and linens, and makes up for space given over to the large window. "I wanted a dressy look," notes the homeowner, and, viewed from the dining room, the pantry appears to be a handsome hutch rather than a wall of cabinets housing a sink, base refrigerator, icemaker, and wine storage unit.

To ensure comfortable proportions in the 19-by-20-foot room with its 14-foot vaulted ceiling, McFarlane and her associate, Gale Kidd, continued the limestone used on the perimeter counter part way up the wall. It is capped with molding to match the frame around the mosaic over the range. To further enhance the room's proportions, they specified 11-inch crown molding and 12-inch baseboards. The floor is also limestone.

Elegant rooms deserve art as well as fine furniture. Above the limestone backsplash, Cottrill hung prints of the monkeys that inspired the design of her chandeliers. She also designed the fish mosaic, which serves as the focal point of the kitchen. "It's like a magnet that draws people across the kitchen," she says. "Everyone wants to touch it."—*Diana King*

Left: A finely crafted armoire with pulls of satin nickel and black horn conceals a pair of Sub-Zero 700 Series refrigerator-freezers. **Right:** The islands are topped with two layers of Norwegian Brown Magic granite laminated together with a double-ogee edge. The black wall cabinet houses a convection oven and television, plus display space and drawers for linens.

cool ideas!

- pullout spice shelves
- adjustable plate racks
- slate message board
- sink built into cooktop

theater in the
round

■ Any designer worth his or her salt strives to make interiors reflect the personalities of his or her clients. In the case of this Beverly Hills kitchen, the wife's French heritage and the husband's desire for substantial materials influenced designer Carla Smith. Moreover, because the kitchen was the starting point for a complete renovation, it had to make a certain statement. "That's why I was inspired to create a kitchen with a Mediterranean feeling," says Smith, the owner of Hub of the House.

"I didn't want the room to look too 'kitcheny,'" she adds. "Rather than fit all the surfaces together, I wanted distinct elements such as the range hood, which gives a really old-world look, and the cooktop, which looks like a piece of furniture."

It also precluded the cookie-cutter look of wall-hung cabinets. Believing that countertop corners are essentially wasted space or at best uncomfortable areas in which to work, Smith created a layout that simply avoids them. The plan consists of two adjacent but independent wall treatments and an island in the shape of a quarter circle. The island houses the main sink, dishwasher, and, in the curve, a commodious breakfast bar.

One wall centers on the cooktop, with an oven installed below. On the other perimeter, a large pantry and a multifunctional

---

A huge skylight centered on a pie-slice-shaped island bathes this Southern California kitchen in sunlight. Cabinets are constructed of a medley of cherry, vertical-grain Douglas fir, and ebony. The stucco range hood is banded in fir sandblasted to accentuate the grain; the floor wears 5-inch-wide planks of vertical-grain Brazilian cherry.

"I used size and shape to relate different elements. The pot rack was based on the refrigerator handle."

cabinet bracket the Sub-Zero Model 632 refrigerator-freezer. The cabinet stores glasses and serving pieces behind glass doors. Because the owners rarely use their microwave, Smith placed it under the toast station. Below it, a warming drawer keeps bread and other prepared foods hot and fresh.

Although Smith wanted to evoke old-world substance, she didn't want to slavishly re-create say, a vintage French farmhouse kitchen, particularly in Southern California. Instead, she opted for a look that's simultaneously warm and contemporary. To achieve this effect, she used a variety of richly textured materials.

Most of the locally made cabinets are cherry with a natural finish accented with touches of sandblasted, vertical-grain Douglas fir. However, in bold contrast, two units are made of ebony. Countertop materials are determined by usage. Most are black Absolute granite, for which Smith specified a honed-matte finish rather than the slick, polished treatment. Veined white Carrera marble appears to the right of the sink.

To shield the sight of dirty dishes in the cleanup area on

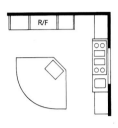

the center island, Smith designed a curved, raised section clad in stainless steel. To the left of the cooktop, oiled teak serves as a chopping surface. To provide the heft that the husband craved, Smith banded the island's curved countertop with a 6-inch-deep apron of teak.

Rather than creating visual chaos, the sum effect of this multimedia approach is harmony, thanks to Smith's attention to proportion and symmetry. "The teak top is 3 inches thick—exactly half the depth of the teak top on the island," she explains. "On either side of the range, a single cabinet of equal width is made of ebony. I also used size and shape to relate different elements. For example, the pot rack's length and diameter were determined by the proportions of the handles on the refrigerator."

This unexpected symphony of materials is visually satisfying, resulting in a kitchen that looks as great as it functions.—*Cathryn Censor*

Left: The island's multiple tasks are defined by its counter surfaces: honed Absolute granite for the cleanup area, stainless for the raised serving area, and teak for the breakfast bar. To the right of the Sub-Zero Model 632 refrigerator-freezer, small appliances stash behind a chalkboard panel operated like a garage door. A warming drawer and microwave, hidden behind a wood panel, sit below.

Above, from left to right: Adjustable dowels hold plates securely, while below, a drawer with mitered corners keeps place mats neatly in place. Vertical-grain Douglas fir "legs" beside the oven pull out to reveal condiments and spices. A stainless-steel sink is an integral component of the cooktop; below, pots have their own dedicated storage space on open shelves.

cool ideas!

- limestone floor
- enameled range
- two ceiling treatments
- granite cottage sink

bigger
is better

■ Legions of homeowners have wrestled with the problem of too little space in the kitchen. But when Clarkston, Michigan, kitchen designer Pamela Bytner-Kilbarger, CKD, of Bytner Design Associates, was called in to work on a 900-plus-square-foot kitchen in a 1920s house, she discovered that an overabundance of space could pose its own set of puzzles. Part of an addition to the French chateau-style residence, the kitchen needed to be both a comfortable family gathering place and a cooking and staging area for large-scale entertaining.

"On one hand, the homeowners wanted a place where they could relax over dinner for two or a morning cup of coffee," says Bytner-Kilbarger. "On the other hand, they needed a kitchen that could accommodate a catering staff and preparations for 250 dinner guests. That's where the challenge lay."

In response, the designer cut the kitchen down to size with a series of subtle visual cues that create separate but overlapping zones. The ceiling, for instance, is divided into a barrel vault over the dining area and a coffered section

In addition to a conventional island, a range with burners and ovens on both sides doubles as a demonstration cooking station for visiting chefs. Anchoring the L-shaped work area, the Sub-Zero Model 650 refrigerator-freezer and Model 601 refrigerator are faced in wood paneling to match the cabinetry.

233

Whether it's dinner for two or 250, this kitchen handles the job with ease.

over the cooking area. The heart of the kitchen is what looks like an island but is actually a custom-made range suite built as one unit. The suite includes burners and ovens on both sides, a sink, a French flat-top burner for making sauces, and a commercial kitchen-style plate rail for resting prepared plates before serving. Behind it is a conventional island with capacious counter space.

An antique wooden table surrounded by upholstered chairs helps to soften the edges of the highly functional space, and provides a comfortable place for dinner parties when the homeowners enjoy cooking with their guests or inviting them to watch a visiting chef prepare a meal.

Two of the kitchen's three Sub-Zero units, including the Model 650 refrigerator-freezer and the Model 601 refrigerator, both in the main cooking area, are paneled to match the cabinetry. The third, a 48-inch-wide Model 632 refrigerator-freezer located in the eating area and used primarily for plating during large catered parties, is clad in stainless steel.

Despite the fact that the kitchen has to stand up to the demands of professional chefs, Bytner-Kilbarger made an effort to keep commercial appliances to a minimum. The ability to camouflage two of the refrigerators, says the designer, "was an important part of the reason for their selection. I wanted to make the kitchen so that the homeowners could come down in the morning and make toast and not feel that they had walked into a commercial kitchen."

Color was Bytner-Kilbarger's secret weapon in taking the institutional edge off the versatile kitchen. Picking up a cue from the style of the rest of the house, she infused the kitchen with a warm Mediterranean palette and striking natural materials. The floor sports creamy limestone, the countertops and moldings are green-toned Costa Smeralda granite, and ceiling beams are crafted of pale natural oak. The range suite is enameled in a rich, sunny yellow. Glossy white paint on the cabinets helps keep the atmosphere light and airy.

The number of cabinets necessary to store the owners' cooking equipment and tableware could have created a daunting wall of doors and drawers. "I used a lot of tricks to avoid monotony," Bytner-Kilbarger says. Wherever possible, cabinets employ glass doors, both to provide visual interest and to display the homeowner's china and glass, which she likes to change seasonally.

Open shelves over one of the kitchen's three sinks show off special serving pieces. Although all are generously proportioned with deep paneling in keeping with the scale of the room, the cabinets are of different heights and dimensions, again to dispel monotony. "They have a lot more girth than typical kitchen cabinet doors," says the designer. "Anything smaller would have been lost in all that space."—*Liz Seymour*

Opposite: The baronial-style antique table is in keeping with the room's 20-foot barrel-vaulted ceiling. The Sub-Zero Model 632 refrigerator-freezer is used primarily for catered events. Twin dishwashers flank the granite apron-front sink. **Above:** A Sub-Zero Model 430 tall wine storage unit is one of two located in the butler's pantry.

rustic
kitchens

If you love the spirit of the outdoors, delight in contrasting textures, and long for simpler times, rustic is *your* style. From a woodsy log cabin to a Colorado ranch and a house built on a rock ledge, these homes feature kitchens that are sure to inspire you. Think massive beamed ceilings, rolling butcher blocks, and granite floors. Imagine stone backsplashes and heavy leaded-glass in cabinet doors. This rough-hewn style has a homey vitality that welcomes friends, neighbors, and family—whether you live in a country lodge or a Connecticut condo.

The limestone tile floor and warm cabinetry are a wonderful contrast to the professional-looking stainless-steel appliances in this restaurant-quality kitchen with rustic appeal.

cool ideas!

- hot-water dispenser
- rough-edged granite
- pot rack with chandelier
- rolling butcher block

home on the
ranch

■ By the time Nancy Lipsky was ready to build her dream home two years ago, she had formulated a clear vision of what she wanted. It helps being in real estate. "I've seen the insides of many of the area houses," she said. "I took a little from here and a little from there."

She and her husband found an ideal spot outside Vail, Colorado, buying 105 acres on a hill overlooking the Sawatch Range. Lipsky laughingly relates, "We call our home Y Knot Ranch because as we decided to do each thing we said, 'Why not?'" The ranch is also home to two yellow Labs, Cassidy and Sundance, as well as a pair of Tennessee Walker horses and two Shetland ponies.

Lipsky turned to architect Duane Piper, of Piper Architects, in Avon, Colorado, and Bob Brownlee, of Cross Creek Contractors in Gypsum, to create a rustic house that looked as though it had been a ranch built in the Colorado Territory, then added on to over time. In those days, Lipsky imagines, her home would have been filled with antiques transported from "back East" in a covered wagon, with local Southwestern pieces added as the living area was expanded.

Opposite: Quirky stools, complete with cowboy boots and even a tail, belly up to the hammered-copper-topped island. The range hood is also copper. To the right of the Sub-Zero Model 650 refrigerator-freezer, a cabinet hides a television. **Above:** Nancy Lipsky and one of her Labs hang out with designer Ricki Brown.

239

The decor suggests a pioneer's dwelling that has been added on to over the years.

When it came to the kitchen, Lipsky discussed her ideas with the architect, then paid a visit to designer Ricki Brown, CKD, of Modern Kitchen Center in Glenwood Springs. "Our starting point was a hammered-copper hood that Nancy had found. It was from a 19th-century Italian villa," says the designer. "We built a chimney for the hood to look like the original."

Hammered copper also appears on the asymmetrical island top, which is edged with clavos, or rivets. The island's base cabinets are painted black with a red underlay coat that occasionally peeks through the distressed finish, picking up the copper hue. A butcher block on casters nestles at one end of the island. At the other end, a prep sink dispenses boiling-hot water for beverages. Overhead, a wrought-iron pot rack doubles as a chandelier, dressed with rawhide shades.

Lipsky selected knotty pine for wall cabinets. "In the old days, they didn't have upper cabinets, so these would have been added later," she says, continuing the illusion that the house has evolved over time. The base cabinets are made of alder with a hand-rubbed barn-red finish, which also appears on a built-in hutch at one end of the room and the tongue-in-groove ceiling supported by a trestle constructed of century-old hand-hewn beams. The floor is reclaimed red oak.

The owner also chose a six-burner professional-style range, a slate-tile backsplash, and a Sub-Zero Model 650 refrigerator-freezer. "I like the Sub-Zero because the freezer and refrigerator have separate compressors," says Brown. The window above the farm sink frames a pasture where horses graze, with aspens and piñon pines beyond. Countertops of Amarello granite are snap-edged, rather than sawn, lending an appropriately raw, rustic look.

A pair of comfortable chairs, one in wicker "that looks like it came off grandma's porch," according to Lipsky, forms a seating area near a cabinet that houses a television. "We watch the news here while we enjoy a glass of wine," she confides.

The kitchen fireplace is clad in the same rusted corrugated metal used for the house's roof. To the right, the breakfast nook boasts more glorious views and the lowered ceiling establishes an intimate atmosphere.

"The kitchen is homey with a sense of vitality that's obvious the moment you walk in," says Brown. For Lipsky, the space is ideal. "You know how people like to gravitate to the kitchen," she says. "We have plenty of space for them to hang out."—*Kathleen Mahoney*

Opposite: The ceiling treatment changes in the breakfast area near the hearth, with its corrugated metal surround. The butcher block rolls out from the island. **Top:** The sitting area's chairs are deliberately mismatched. The bar sink dispenses instant hot water. **Above left:** Cabinets made of pine are lightly stained to keep them from yellowing. **Above right:** A Y-shaped iron bracket with a knot under the counter is a visual pun on the ranch's name.

cool ideas!

- "wine cellar" doors on fridges
- powder-coated steel counters
- fire-clay farmhouse sink
- perforated-metal door insets

best of the west

■ Pamela and Phillip Kurtz, of Haworth of England by Pamela, faced several extraordinary challenges when they took on the design of the 600-square-foot kitchen in a spacious log house in Telluride, Colorado. Though the house is new, the owners desired a rustic and natural "Old West" decor to blend with the architecture, rugged location, and dramatic views from their vacation home.

Part of the challenge was to devise a kitchen that not only functioned well and included every modern convenience, but that looked as though it had been built before such labor-saving appliances even existed. And the designers had to pull all this off long distance, working from their Connecticut location with a cabinetmak-

Left: Adjacent to the kitchen, a cozy seating nook centers on a river rock fireplace, one of several in the house. **Right:** Liberal use of such natural materials as stone; ash floors; painted, stained, and distressed oak cabinetry; and hand-forged metal strap hardware reinforce the illusion that this ski-lodge kitchen has been around for decades.

"The refrigerator door panels recess into a channel cut into the adjoining log walls."

er based in England and a builder in Colorado.

"We built this house large enough to be comfortable even when another family the size of ours is visiting—and we have three young children," says the wife. So the kitchen had to follow suit, easily accommodating a crowd. The open floor plan means the kitchen is at the core of the living space and visible from adjoining areas.

In response, Pamela designed the cabinetry to look like furniture. Inspiration for the cabinet finish came from a piece of antique oak flooring the client had found. The cabinetmakers matched the look with English oak, specifically selected for its cracks and unique character. "We're especially pleased that the cabinets have a homey and comfortable feel, like armoires and cupboards built or collected over time," says the owner.

"The key to the success of the design was concealing all the appliances except the range and the microwave," explains Pamela. While the eight-burner professional-style gas range with two ovens is highlighted with a backsplash of rustic slate tiles and an oak, steel, and stucco range hood, the rest of the appliances are camouflaged behind panels that match the cabinets. It takes a discerning eye to find the dishwasher

Top right: The microwave is located out of the main flow of traffic but still convenient to snack items stored behind perforated-metal mesh doors in a cabinet designed to look like an antique cupboard. **Right:** Just around the corner from the kitchen, this hutch was hand-painted and distressed by the cabinetmakers to match the base of the island, helping to unify the open-plan spaces.

to the left of the main farmhouse sink and a trash compactor to the right. But the most remarkable feature is the cleverly concealed refrigeration. Two 30-inch-wide Sub-Zero Model 611 refrigerator-freezers were installed side by side and then fitted with overlay panels disguised to mimic the doors to a wine cellar. "They are hidden so well that we joke if we weren't there to show them, our visitors wouldn't be able to find any food," says the owner.

The designers had not previously worked with logs, which present unique challenges. "The job became more technical because of the log walls," says Phillip. Over time, logs compress from their own weight. Therefore, the refrigerator enclosure had to be designed to accommodate the required 2-inch vertical shrinkage and compression of the log walls. Moreover, it had to still allow the oversize overlay panels to open, without hitting the frame of the enclosure or the appliances themselves.

Phillip built a scale model to ensure that the overlay panel door design would work. "The panels recess into a channel cut into the adjoining log walls so the logs can shrink and compress without crushing any of the facade or the refrigerators," he notes. "Sub-Zero is the only company that makes provision for an overlay application."

Top left: The eight-burner, two-oven range can serve a crowd. The slate backsplash, iron strapping, and chalet-style wood accents on the range hood extend the rustic theme.
Left: Flanked by log walls, two Sub-Zero Model 611 refrigerator-freezers hide behind custom-made overlay panels. One unit is hinged on the left, the other on the right.

"The cabinets look like armoires and cupboards collected over time."

Another important feature of the open-plan design is the roughly 10-by-7-foot island. A roomy L-shaped snack bar on the dining room side of the island seats seven comfortably. The granite-topped work-height countertop houses a second sink.

The cabinets that form the base of the island were hand painted black and distressed. (Perimeter cabinets wear a light stain.) And the cabinetry in the island conceals a Sub-Zero icemaker and a wine storage unit opposite the main refrigerators.

Other carefully chosen materials support the rustic look. The ceiling is clad in natural pine, fireplaces are con-structed of river rock, and a fire-clay farmhouse sink is fitted with weathered copper-and-brass faucets. The perimeter countertop is charcoal-colored powder-coated steel. Handmade and hand-welded, it is ⅛ inch thick. Throughout the house, wide-plank ash floors were hand-distressed on site.

Much of the decorative hardware—including the light fixtures, the strap hinges on the doors that conceal the refrigerators, the wall sconces, and the fireplace doors and screens—were handcrafted by a local blacksmith. With such technical ingenuity, craftsmanship and vision, the Old West lives on.—*Elaine Martin Petrowski*

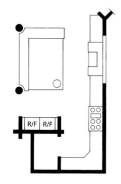

Left: The snack bar is adjacent to the dining area. The ceiling is covered with natural pine planking. All posts and beams are made of pine. **Right:** The farmhouse sink is made of fire clay. All appliances, including a trash compactor to the right of the sink and a dishwasher to its left, are concealed with wood panels.

- stucco range hood
- stone wall behind cooktop
- turned legs on island
- plank inset in butcher block

out of the WOODS

■ This 13-by-21-foot kitchen in Fargo, North Dakota, started life with an architectural given: a fieldstone wall left standing when the previous building on the site was razed to construct a French country-style home. The backside of a fireplace, the wall was the logical spot for the cooktop and vent hood, but was not centered in the room.

Kitchen designer Tricia Hauser Tidemann of North Star Kitchens addressed the problem by framing the cooktop and copper-tile-banded range hood with a pair of glass-fronted wall cabinets. Like a picture frame, the cabinets impose symmetry. Suspending the copper pot rack over the center island directly in front of the range also helps correct the picture.

Hauser Tidemann's second design challenge was to make the large room feel cozy when the clients entertain there. "Because it is an open-plan kitchen, we concealed most appliances behind wood-paneled cabinet doors," Hauser Tidemann says. "The Sub-Zero 700 Series refrigerator and freezer units are ideal." A two-drawer 700 Series refrigerator installed by the secondary sink in the 7-by-10-foot island aids in salad preparation.

Wood predominates in cabinetry, flooring, ceiling beams, and the island counter, relieved by a tumbled marble backsplash and granite counters of beige with a blush of salmon-pink. Alder cabinets wear a crackle finish in warm brown for perimeter units and olive-green for the island. Happily, the room's traditional styling made no concessions to efficiency.—*B.M.*

Left: Massive turned-wood legs and a plank of teak inset in the teak end-grain butcher block define the snack bar area of the island. The curved bonnet above the fridge and freezer, the stucco range hood, and gleaming copper accents lend a rustic French look.
Right: The porcelain farm sink is mounted in a cabinet whose carved toe-kick suggests fine furniture.

cool ideas!

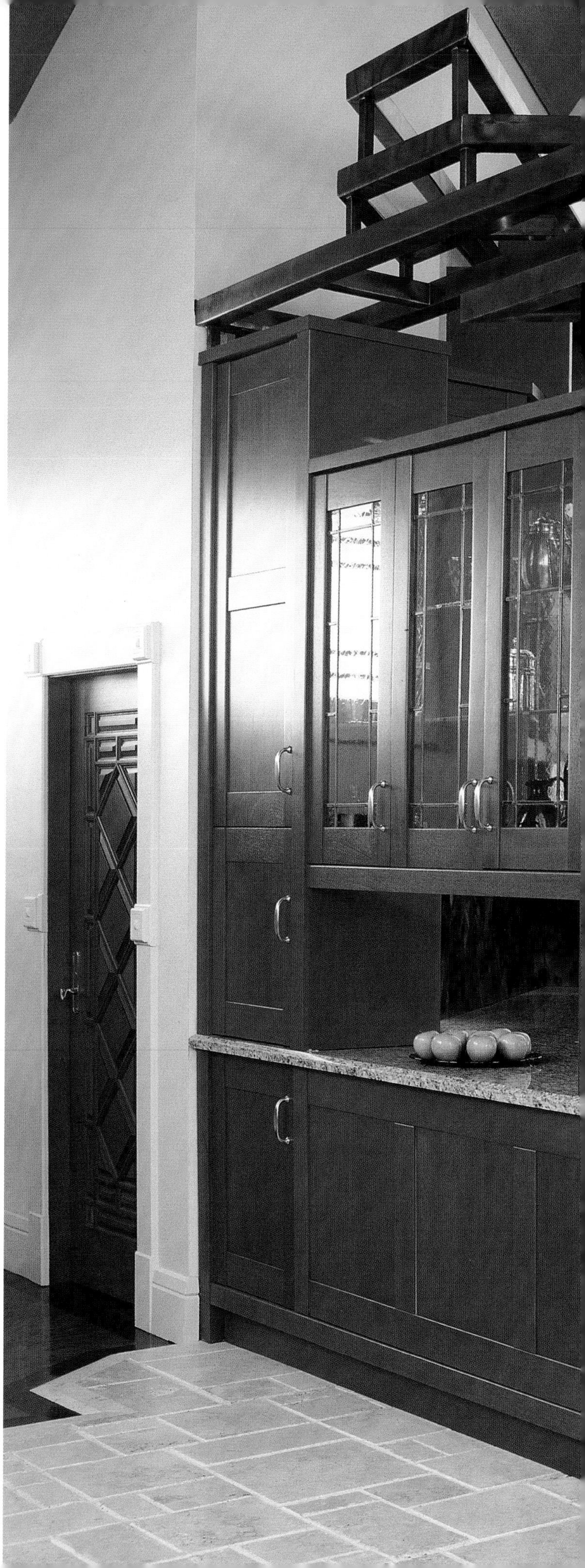

- toe-kick lighting
- leaded glass in cabinets
- flamed stainless steel
- octagonal butcher block

reach for the skies

■ The word "unique" is often misapplied, but not in the case of this kitchen that sits like a jewel inside a massive great-room in an extraordinary new house built into a rock ledge. With its lodgelike styling and soaring ceilings, you might expect to find this home in the "Big Sky Country" of the far West. In actuality, it was built in Greenwich, Connecticut.

The owner, described by his kitchen designers as "a risk taker," is a bachelor who works as a manufacturing consultant and enjoys entertaining large groups in his one-of-kind residence. He wanted both the house and its kitchen "to be like nothing you have ever seen," says Terry Scarborough, CMKBD, ASID. She, Walter Grabowski, CKD, and Carrie Deane Corcoran, all of Kitchens by Deane, designed the project.

The planning and construction of the house were as complex as the design itself, taking approximately three years to complete. The kitchen was in the design-and-build stage for a little less than a year, and the designers even built a scale model of the kitchen before proceeding with actual construction. The 14-by-22-foot kitchen is set into the family room, which at its

Like an immense octagonal sculpture of wood, metal, and stone, the kitchen occupies a portion of a huge family room. Glass in cabinets echoes the leading in the 16-foot-tall windows.

PHOTOGRAPHY: CHRISTOPHER HORNSBY

"At night the kitchen feels like it's suspended in space."

highest point soars 26 feet to meet a ceiling of graceful curved wood panels. The space also serves as a dining room and includes a massive octagonal dining table made of an exotic African hardwood.

Everything about this kitchen is overscaled, including some of the kitchen cabinets, which tower to 15 feet. Intriguingly, there is only one rather narrow means of entry into the kitchen proper. "Another opening might have made for easier access from other parts of the room, but the client prefers having the kitchen remain a separate enclave," explains Scarborough.

In consultation with their client, the designers selected ruggedly luxurious materials. The house's rocky setting is recalled in granite counters and the floor of limestone blocks set in an intricate cobblestone pattern. The backsplash and custom-designed range hood are torch-flamed stainless steel.

The process, referred to as "oil canning" by metalsmiths, discolors and slightly texturizes and warps the metal, which then acquires a patina that appears to change as the light shifts throughout the day. Together with the superstructure needed to support it, the hood becomes a kind of free-form sculpture. Flamed stainless is also used on the backsplash, where it adds even more highlights and softens any suggestion of a cool look.

The mahogany cabinets have leaded-glass inserts reminiscent of Arts and Crafts styling and appropriate to the home's lodge style. Mahogany fronts allow the Sub-Zero Model 632 side-by-side refrigerator-freezer to blend into the decor. "The owner wanted the largest combination unit available for maximum storage and this 48-inch-wide unit fits nicely into the available space," says Scarborough.

All in all, the mahogany's deep tones, the textures of stone, and the patina of the flamed stainless steel impart great warmth and drama to the room. No less than four different lighting sources contribute. There is cathode lighting in the ceiling for general illumination, halogen lighting in the range hood and in undercabinet fixtures, and special effects lighting in glass-fronted cabinets and at toe-kick level. "At night, when the toe-kick lighting is on, the kitchen feels as if it's suspended in space," marvels Scarborough.—*B.M.*

Opposite: The octagonal chopping block repeats the shape of the kitchen itself. Toe-kick lighting contributes safety and drama. The stainless-steel backsplash is quilted, then flamed. **Above:** The 48-inch-wide overlay Sub-Zero refrigerator-freezer is fully integrated with the rest of the cabinets. A reverse vaulted ceiling extends over the room. **Right:** The range hood is custom made. Counters are granite, the floor limestone.

ethnic kitchens

Whether you hark to the call of African drumbeats, brilliant Mediterranean colors, or calm Asian simplicity, there's an ethnic decor sure to suit your personality. This look is the tastiest dish yet from the global melting pot. So go ahead and add a cultural accent to your kitchen. Use a Mexican serape for a tablecloth, or dramatize an ancient monastery door as a focal point. The kitchens on the pages ahead will show you how to express yourself in a wide range of exotic styles that are as festive as they are functional.

A refrigerator-freezer and tall freezer flank the main work areas of this kitchen for convenience and accessibility. Metal inserts in some of the cabinet doors dramatically echo the stainless-steel appliances—while zigzag motifs on other doors speak to the American Southwest. See page 268 for more on this kitchen.

DESIGNER: KATHY JACKSON; PHOTOGRAPHY: © ROBERT RECK

cool ideas!

- bamboo flooring
- pair of islands
- Japanese storage chest
- honed-slate counters

pacific calm

PHOTOGRAPHY: BRIAN GRIFFIN, STYLING: TRICE BOERENS

■ Designer Earl A. Miller of Arendal Kitchen Design says he "gets excited when people ask for something a little different." His pulse must have quickened considerably when he first saw a recent project: A new home fashioned after a Japanese temple and boasting an indoor pool. Remarkable by any standard, its setting in Layton, Utah, made it all the more unusual.

Long before ground was broken for construction, the owners, two doctors—she is of Japanese descent—had called in a Feng Shui expert to determine the best location and orientation. Now, with the completed house poised handsomely over a creek, the couple turned the same exacting attention to the interior.

Wishing to extend the Asian theme into the kitchen, they asked for natural materials such as wood, glass, and stone and left the rest to Miller.

One of the first design challenges he and associate Jody Theobald faced was the space itself. The 13-by-14-foot kitchen—part of a great-room roughly 60 feet square with a two-story vaulted ceiling—felt cavernous and cold. Also, while sunlight was abundant in most of the great-room, the kitchen proper had no direct source of light.

Miller relied on the layout of cabinetry to define the kitchen and make it feel intimate. Two islands, one primarily for eating and another for prep work, divide the space into distinct areas without impeding traffic flow.

The main island houses a sink, clear storage bins, drawers, and a dishwasher. The "snack bar" island neatly divides kitchen space from the adjoining great-room. More than just a place to eat, the snack bar has a Sub-Zero 700 Series base refrigerated drawer unit that lets the couple's children help themselves to beverages and snacks. A second dishwasher and bar sink make for easy cleanup; cookbooks and wine are both stored in this island as well.

"The two islands allow both homeowners to cook simultaneously without getting in each other's way," explains

Left: The Sub-Zero 700 Series base refrigerator is housed in the secondary island. The pocket door to the left of the antique tansu chest leads to the indoor pool. **Right:** The central prep island has two levels to accommodate cooks of different heights. The countertop is made of honed slate.

"Too many upper cabinets give a kitchen a confining feel."

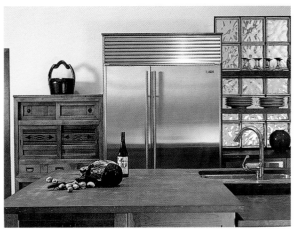

Miller. "The person at the prep island can be in the main work triangle while someone else at the snack bar island can move back and forth from the refrigerated drawers to the cooktop without colliding with the main cook on the way to the primary refrigerator."

The kitchen shares one wall with a pool room studded with skylights. By installing glass block on a portion of the party wall, Miller was able to "steal" light from this space. Artificial illumination in the form of recessed cans in the ceiling and lights installed under wall-hung cabinets contribute general and task lighting.

To bring needed warmth to the kitchen, Miller relied on materials rich in texture and color. Appropriately, the floor is made of strips of laminated bamboo. Its blonde, mottled appearance gives a sun-dappled look to the room.

Honed-slate countertops—hardrock maple is used on the snack bar island—and forged iron pulls provide a rough-hewn charm. In contrast, glass block and stainless-steel appliances, including the Sub-Zero Model 632 refrigerator-freezer, provide contemporary sleekness.

"The owners wanted stainless steel for the appliances because they like that industrial look," says Miller. "I specified Sub-Zero because the company has been around forever and I like to go with an old reliable when I can."

To match an antique Japanese tansu chest, Miller selected cabinets in a natural cherry finish. And to give the kitchen an unfitted look, he limited the number of wall cabinets. "Too many upper cabinets give a kitchen a confining feel," he comments. "Besides, who says you have to keep your dishes and glassware in an upper cabinet? Rules are meant to be broken."

And here is another interesting observation. "If you take away some of the Asian accessories," says the designer, "this kitchen could have a completely different look. With the plain panel-fronted cabinets and natural finishes, it's a very versatile kitchen."—C.C.

Left: The kitchen proper is partially distinguished from the great-room by cedar posts. Minimal use of wall-hung cabinets adds to the serene atmosphere. **Top:** Beside the stainless-steel Sub-Zero Model 632 refrigerator-freezer, a "window" of glass block borrows light from other rooms. **Above:** Clear bins store nonperishable foods. The choice of forged-iron pulls was inspired by the hardware on the tansu chest.

cool ideas!

- hand-carved woodwork
- glass peephole to pantry
- distressed painted finish
- concealed microwave

ancient
echoes

■ No cookie-cutter kitchen for these homeowners! "I faced a unique design challenge when my clients wanted every corner of this kitchen to contain an element of authentic, Southwest-style architecture, an uncommon request in Florida," says kitchen designer Jackie Bentley Brown, of The Olde World Cabinet Company.

The 560-square-foot kitchen was part of a newly constructed house outside Orlando. So convincing is the illusion, that the kitchen could seamlessly fit into a house in Mexico or the American Southwest.

The room's inspiration began years earlier, when one of the homeowners fell in love with the sturdy lines and warm materials used in the houses built by Spanish settlers in Mexico and New Mexico. The couple, both frequent travelers and cooks, researched the details for their home for several years before starting to build.

As the wife studied books on Southwest architecture, she found herself inexplicably drawn to the carved door panels in an ancient monastery built in the 1700s in

Rough-hewn pine panels front the tall Sub-Zero 700 Series refrigerator and freezer, suggesting a pair of antique hand-carved cupboards. Next to the fridge, a cabinet stores canned goods and a microwave. Plaster walls, a beamed ceiling, and terra-cotta tile contribute to the Mexican style.

PHOTOGRAPHY: © KIM SARGENT, SARGENT ARCHITECTURAL PHOTOGRAPHY; STYLING: GINA COOKE-SCOTT

"We painted the island cobalt blue, then distressed it for added drama."

Zacatecas, a historic northern Mexican town. Those carvings became the focal point of this unusual kitchen.

Brown hired a local artisan to replicate the elaborate carvings that now adorn key parts of the kitchen, supplying him with a book on Mexican history and architecture for inspiration. One piece of his handiwork can be found in the intricately carved wood trim that skirts the bottom of the plaster range hood.

More custom carvings grace the grainy, rough-hewn, quartersawn pine panels and doors used throughout the kitchen. Two identical panels—carved with cherub, animal, and floral motifs—front the tall Sub-Zero 700 Series refrigerator and freezer that flank an arched niche.

To the right of the refrigerator, a built-in cabinet cleverly houses a microwave accessed by flipping up a retractable door. Next to the professional-style range is a butler's pantry hidden by another carved, arched doorway. Here, a bubbled-glass insert mimics the look of an old monastery door. After the intricate carvings were executed, the doors and cabinets were distressed, then glazed, to achieve an authentic antique impression.

Pristine white plaster walls set off the dark pine cabinetry. "It's unusual to find plaster walls in new homes in Florida," says Brown. "However, some houses that date from the 1920s were built with plaster walls. It costs more to use plaster, but it helps keep the house cool."

In keeping with traditional Spanish architecture, the kitchen has few wall cabinets. Instead, built-in cupboards hold dishes and packaged goods. More decorative items are displayed on the arched shelf backed with colorful, custom-painted tiles.

A pair of plaster-framed cubby drawers to either side of the oven holds cooking utensils. Two wall-mounted leaded-glass-fronted cabinets—also distressed and glazed to coordinate with the pantry doors and panels on the Sub-Zeros—are mounted on either side of the window over the sink.

"The homeowners have a fabulous eye for creating dramatic color combinations," acknowledges Brown. "I've never seen anything like the granite my client found to put on top of the island and around the sink," she says of the peachy-coral stone with cobalt-blue veining.

"To complement the blue in the granite, we painted the island cobalt blue, then distressed it to bring even more drama to the room." The Mexican Saltillo tile floor ties together the entire south-of-the-border scheme and creates an inviting foundation for this unique kitchen.—*M.Z.S.*

Above: The carved wood trim skirting the plaster range hood was copied from a Mexican monastery. Tiles are custom painted.
Right: The Sub-Zero 700 Series refrigerator offers two pullout drawers.
Opposite: Wainscot panels, carved feet and pilasters, and a kneehole covered in beaded board make the island look like furniture. The paint was distressed, then glazed.

cool ideas!

- appliance armoire
- mantel over range
- peaked arches
- mosaic-lined niches

exotic ambience

■ This Florida kitchen could be a case-book study in cultural fusion. It also demonstrates the benefits of teamwork. "The design was a collaborative effort among the builder, interior designer Grant Eric Gribble, of Gribble Interior Group, and myself," observes kitchen designer Cassandra K. Walters, CKD, of Central Kitchen & Bath in Winter Park, Florida. "Our goal was to create a kitchen for more than one cook and to facilitate entertaining."

The house was used as a showhouse to benefit the Orlando Opera Guild. During the construction phase, the plans were reviewed by a family with two children, who fell in love with it and decided to purchase it before it was even completed. Fortuitously, the planned kitchen perfectly suited their needs.

Because the 234-square-foot space is open to the great-room, eye appeal was a must. "We wanted to create a kitchen with an Eastern-Mediterranean style that also would be a functional work space," says Walters.

The Mediterranean styling of the home reflects the architecture typical of central Florida in the 1920s and 30s. Arches—some with simple curved tops, and other, complex Moorish ones that culminate in points—vibrant colors, niches to display pottery, and decorative ceiling elements, such as the wood beams in the adjacent great-room, establish the exotic ambience. So do the 15-foot ceilings, extensive use of limestone in columns that frame the armoire and windows, and tiled walls and floor.

Despite its old-world manners, the kitchen is equally conversant in 21st-century efficiency. Though filled with state-of-the-art appliances, the key to establishing the Eastern Mediterranean ambience is the concealing of some of the units or making them unobtrusive. "We selected the Sub-Zero 700 Series to pull off this disappearing act," Walters explains. "Instead of two refrigerator-freezers standing side by side, you see a walnut armoire."

Walters also selected a professional-style 48-inch-wide Wolf range because, she says, "The combination of six burners, a griddle, and two ovens is every serious cook's dream." To integrate the range into the Mediterranean theme, it is graced with a walnut mantel complete with corbels supporting a limestone-faced hood. Built-in shelves above the range store condiments. A microwave and two dishwashers, plus a Sub-Zero

Above: The walnut armoire conceals a Sub-Zero 700 Series tall refrigerator and freezer. **Opposite:** A Moorish archway connects kitchen and great-room. Windows are accented with spiral limestone pilasters, matching those flanking the armoire, and topped with glass mosaics.

The compact kitchen is the envy of caterers.

wine storage unit in a pantry, complete the suite of appliances.

Despite its modest size, the home-owners find the space eminently work-able. "It gives my husband and me lots of room to work at the same time," says the wife. The kitchen in their old home was much larger, she adds, but they used to get in each other's way. No more: Two sinks, one below the windows and another in the island, define distinct work areas.

The kitchen is also a caterer's dream. "The island and eating-bar counters are frequently used for buffet arrange-ments," she adds. "Caterers often com-ment that they wish they had such a nice kitchen for their own businesses!"

True to the old-world theme, all the custom cabinetry has a rich furniture look. Perimeter cabinets of knotty pine wear a lighter finish than do the darker, walnut appliance armoire and range mantel. Teal paint on the maple cabi-nets that make up the island alludes to the color of the great-room walls. Green accents recur in Verdi Peacock granite counters, which display pearlescent chips in dark green and black marbling.

The attention to detail displayed throughout this space is a testament to the fact that even a small kitchen can be efficient and welcoming. It can also be wonderfully exotic.—*Wanda Jankowski*

Right: Living-room looks are essential in a kitchen visible from the front door. The raised eating bar serves as a visual barrier. **Left:** The limestone range-hood treatment, walnut mantel, and backsplash adorned with rusticated-limestone tiles make the Wolf range a focal point. Turned columns give the granite-topped island the look of fine furniture.

cool ideas!

- lightening-bolt motif
- zigzag soffit trim
- hand-painted tiles
- concrete floor
- custom cat door

southwestern
revival

■ Near the banks of the Rio Grande in Albuquerque, New Mexico, is a new adobe house designed by architects Lee Shaw and Rick Ansaldi, of Ansaldi/Shaw Design in Tucson. The exterior, complete with a tall structure that suggests a Mission bell tower, captures the look of old New Mexico. The challenge for Ansaldi and Shaw was to update the adobe aesthetic to meet the owners' request for a contemporary kitchen full of color and character. Kitchen designer Kathy Jackson, of J. Wheeler & The Branch Cabinetry in Albuquerque, took over from there to make a beautiful design even more beautiful in its practicality. Because the kitchen is accessed from three different rooms, Jackson paid careful attention to the traffic pattern. "I kept the aisles

Left: The Sub-Zero Model 642 refrigerator-freezer and 700 Series tall freezer flank the main work areas. Metal inserts in some of the cabinet doors reference the appliances' stainless-steel cladding. **Opposite:** The carved door, lightning-bolt cabinet panels, and corner posts of the island are all traditional Southwestern elements. A skylight in front of the plaster archway contributes natural light.

The kitchen meets everyone's needs, even the four-footed members of the family.

wide and laid out the room so that people can walk through the kitchen to the family room without interfering with the work area," she explains.

The homeowners, a couple with a teenage daughter, like to cook as a family. In response, Jackson established two distinct yet overlapping work triangles, each anchored by the Sub-Zero Model 642 refrigerator-freezer. The cooking triangle includes a 48-inch-wide cooktop, two wall ovens, and a double stainless-steel sink in the island. The food preparation triangle includes another double stainless-steel sink, as well as a built-in microwave. The Sub-Zero 700 Series tall freezer conveniently stores frozen foods nearby. There are also two dishwashers and two warming drawers.

Decorative elements in the kitchen draw inspiration from several sources. "The owners saw a photograph in a Santa Fe museum by Jesse Nusbaum, a mid-20th-century archaeologist and photographer for the National Park Service, who studied ancient Southwestern civilizations," says Jackson. "They wanted design elements from that photo to be reflected in the kitchen. We incorporated the contemporary lightning-bolt motif in the custom maple cabinetry and twisted carved corner posts of the island."

In her pursuit of color, the homeowner selected the hand-painted tiles that appear in the kitchen and throughout the rest of the house with Jenny Lind of Rainbow Gate, in Santa Fe. Lilac-tinted window frames contribute additional strokes of color to the

Near right: In the breakfast area, the built-in plaster *banco* has a sloped back for seating comfort. The table overlooks the patio, which includes an outdoor kitchen. A serape and rustic chair add colorful notes.

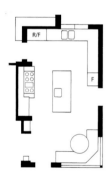

interior. Contemporary textural elements include the earth-toned concrete floor, the granite countertops, and stainless-steel screen inserts in several of the maple cabinet doors.

Updates on traditional New Mexican styling appear in the plaster archway that frames the cooktop area and the echoing tiled arch beneath the cooktop. Seeded-glass inserts adorn the upper portions of the wall cabinets. Painted a soft green, the vintage-look beaded-board ceiling carries through to the adjoining butler's pantry.

As well as offering additional storage and space for the washer and dryer, the butler's pantry is the feeding station for the family's cats and dog. Litter boxes hide in cabinets beneath the pantry sink, accessible through a whimsical cutout in a pair of doors.

The kitchen's 12-foot ceiling features an ample skylight in front of the archway that frames the cooktop area. A pair of windows over the main sink that overlooks the entry courtyard brings in additional light, as does another window over the eating *banco* that furnishes a view into the rear patio. In the evening, illumination comes from recessed downlights in the ceiling and cobalt-blue pendants suspended above the island.

"What I enjoy most is that although it's a big kitchen, it's an efficient space," says the homeowner, who is not only the primary cook, but has also acted as a contractor herself. "I worked with superb designers and all of them were committed to the project."—*Wanda Jankowski*

Above: The semicircular tiled alcove beneath the cooktop mimics the archway above it. **Above right:** In the butler's pantry, a playful cutout accesses the cats' litter boxes.

cool ideas!

- recycled antique pieces
- cabinets inspired by a fence
- mix of stone surfaces
- single punch of bold color

the ▪ flavor of
java

▪ "My clients had planned a trip to Indonesia that had to be canceled," explains architect R. Stephen Chauvin of Metaire, Louisiana. "So when we started planning their kitchen renovation, we decided to bring in as many Indonesian elements as we could." The name of Chauvin's firm, Arkhitekton, Inc., incorporates the Greek words *arkhi*, meaning hand or chief, and *tekton*, meaning builder. This concept reflects his design and build philosophy, meaning he is involved in every aspect of execution. This kitchen's cabinets are a case in point.

"What inspired our cabinet design was a piece of hand-carved teak fencing we found in an antiques shop," Chauvin says. He ordered the Indonesian piece cut and shaped to shroud a stainless-steel exhaust hood. The way the wood was used in this fencing, particularly the tall vertical slats, established the design theme for the cabinets crafted of Spanish cedar.

Soapstone tops the dining peninsula, Inca Gold limestone tops the island, and Sahara Gold granite tops the cabinets beside the black-and-brass French LaCanache range. Industrial-style equipment would have been out of place in this kitchen. The cabinets complement an antique Indonesian fence in front of the range hood. The cabinet to the left hides a television and microwave.

"The cabinet design was inspired by a piece of hand-carved teak found in an antiques shop."

"The look of the kitchen has very little to do with the architecture of the house, which was built in a suburb of New Orleans shortly before the second World War," Chauvin explains. The owners desired an exotic look. Hence the glazed walls—yellow stippled with orange creates a rich mustard color—and the vivid blue-green window trim, all of which help transform the space from chilly 1980s Euro style to the tropics' timeless warmth.

"We worked within the existing shell," he points out, "but we gutted nearly everything in that space." The architect immediately closed off one doorway, turned part of a bay window into a door, and did away with a space-consuming pantry. He also designed a series of work areas that would allow more than one person to cook at a time and, at the same time, underscore a sense of intimacy. To compensate for the loss of the pantry, Chauvin placed a tall cabinet across from the peninsula. The cabinet opens to display a tele-

---

Left: An antique Indonesian panel defines the breakfast area. Walls that mimic the framework around the panel were faux-painted. One opening of the three-window bay became a French door. **Above:** The ceiling's faux beams separate antique pine slats arranged in a chevron pattern. Ironstone sinks with a tortoiseshell glaze are mounted over the granite countertop. The chandelier is a French antique.

"In some ways a kitchen can be a more intimate space than a bedroom."

vision, coffee maker, and microwave, plus ample shelves for food storage. Double doors retract so as not to impede traffic flow.

Antique-look 8-inch-square floor tiles laid diagonally unify the varied elements of this L-shaped kitchen—and also echo the diagonal pattern on the ceiling. Black soapstone forms a backsplash behind the range and covers the peninsula between kitchen and breakfast areas; Sahara Gold granite tops all other counters except for that on the island, which wears Inca Gold limestone.

"I love kitchens," says Chauvin. "Each can be the most wonderful space in a home, and in some ways is more intimate than the bedroom. Even clients not fond of cooking tend to use

their kitchen. That's why I try to make it an extension of the things they love. Sub-Zero helps me do that. No other product of comparable quality has the same potential for integration." He built in the 700 Series refrigerator and freezer behind cedar cabinet doors.

Details work hand in glove with design to make this exotic kitchen beautiful as well as functional. The wood ceiling in the kitchen and woven-cane mat ceiling in the breakfast area complete an aura of coziness. The cabinetry, much of which was designed to resemble a series of small drawers, actually includes wide bins and deep drawers that hold every conceivable cooking need.

Cabinet hardware is a contemporary fabrication of several antique designs, all in brass that's been given a tarnished look. The appliances, either understated in design or cleverly concealed, never intrude. "This room doesn't scream 'kitchen!'" boasts Chauvin.—*M.K.*

It's an open-and-shut case. A tall 700 Series Sub-Zero refrigerator tucks behind Spanish cedar doors to the left of the range. On the adjacent wall, a coordinated freezer sits beside Sub-Zero's undercounter wine storage unit—with separate controls for red and white wines. Both fridge and freezer wear elongated door handles cast from an antique brass pull.

Kitchen Planning Kit

■ Now that you've had an opportunity to tour dozens of expertly designed kitchens, it's time to transform your kitchen dreams into an achievable reality—and this planning kit is here to help!

Even if you choose to hire a team of designers, architects, and contractors to put your dreams in motion, it is recommended that you sketch out some ideas. And, if you don't consider yourself an artist, don't worry: Your drawings will better help you envision the kitchen you're after, and it will prove invaluable as you begin to share you vision with the professionals.

When you begin to plan your ideal kitchen, use the spaces featured throughout the book as a guide: By looking at how these kitchens function, what type of kitchen they are (fit for entertaining, for serious cooking, or for intimate evenings for two), and traffic flow, for example, you'll be able to better visualize how you want your very own kitchen to look and feel. As you think about these big-picture considerations, also envision any architectural features you'd like to add or highlight and what types, sizes, and styles of appliances, cabinetry, shelving, and furnishings you want to include.

Plot your kitchen using the grid on page 281 (1 square equals 1 square foot of floor space), taking into consideration any pantry, entry, mudroom, office, dining area, or bump-outs you'd like to add to your home or remodel at the same time.

Use the architectural symbols below to mark the position of existing architectural features. Use a different color to indicate added features, such as the placement of built-ins and furniture. Use dotted lines to mark obstructions, including prominent light fixtures and angled ceilings. Keep in mind that one of the keys to making your kitchen both functional and beautiful is good placement of doors, windows, appliances, cabinetry, islands, and built-in features, so consider these elements as you plan.

Use the templates on pages 278–280 to experiment with different placements for furniture, appliances, and built-in features. Trace or photocopy the appropriate items from the templates and cut them out with a crafts knife or scissors. If you desire specialty furniture or other features, such as a peninsula or an island, measure and draw them to the same scale (1 square equals 1 square foot) on the grid paper.

Architectural Symbols

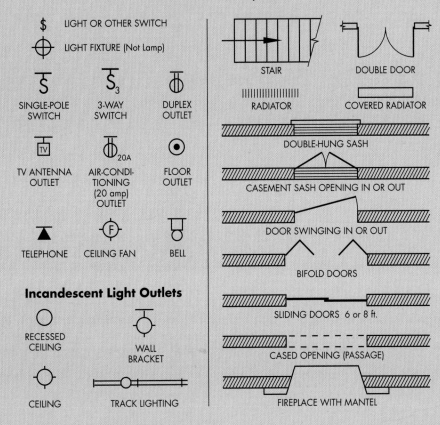

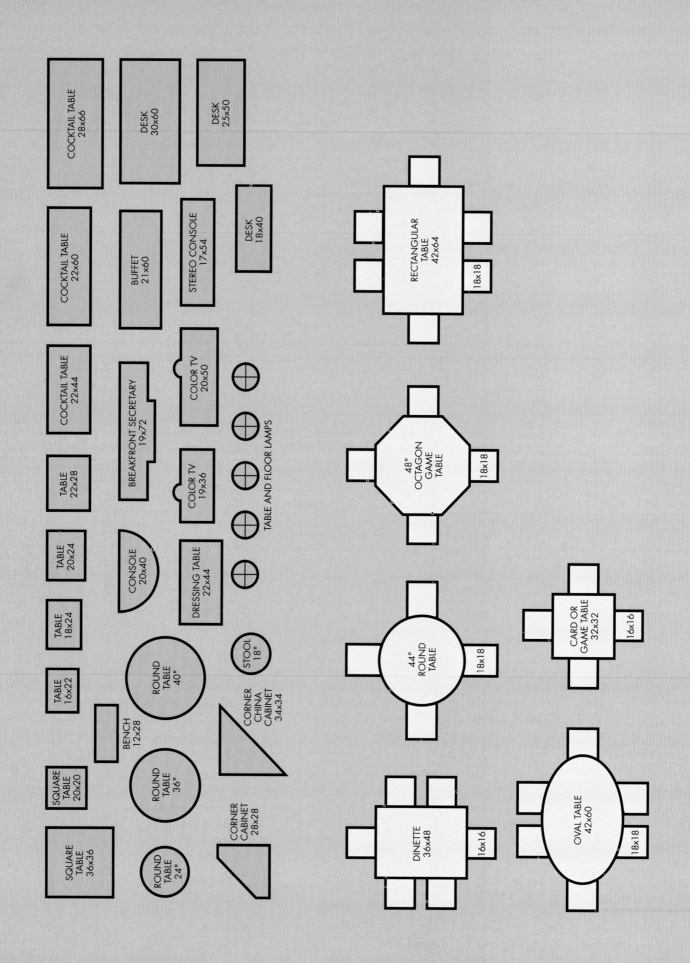

COCKTAIL TABLE
28x66

DESK
30x60

DESK
25x50

COCKTAIL TABLE
22x60

BUFFET
21x60

STEREO CONSOLE
17x54

DESK
18x40

COCKTAIL TABLE
22x44

BREAKFRONT SECRETARY
19x72

COLOR TV
20x50

TABLE
22x28

COLOR TV
19x36

TABLE
20x24

CONSOLE
20x40

DRESSING TABLE
22x44

TABLE AND FLOOR LAMPS

TABLE
18x24

TABLE
16x22

ROUND TABLE
40"

STOOL
18"

BENCH
12x28

CORNER CHINA CABINET
34x34

SQUARE TABLE
20x20

ROUND TABLE
3'6"

SQUARE TABLE
36x36

ROUND TABLE
24"

CORNER CABINET
28x28

RECTANGULAR TABLE
42x64
18x18

48"
OCTAGON GAME TABLE
18x18

44"
ROUND TABLE
18x18

CARD OR GAME TABLE
32x32
16x16

DINETTE
36x48
16x16

OVAL TABLE
42x60
18x18

Kitchen Planning Kit

Base Cabinets

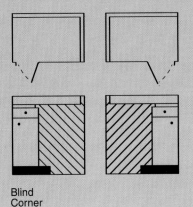

Blind
Corner

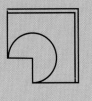

Lazy Susan
Angle

Lazy Susan
Corner

Cabinetry

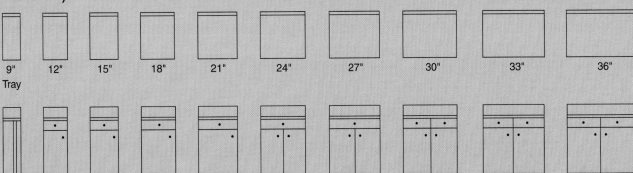

| 9" | 12" | 15" | 18" | 21" | 24" | 27" | 30" | 33" | 36" |

Tray

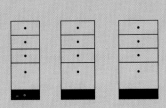

Sink Bases

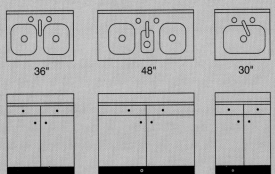

36"   48"   30"

Using Templates

Use the templates on pages 278–280 to mark the placement of common kitchen components. The templates include both plan-view ("top-down") and elevation ("side view") perspectives, allowing you to create both floor plans and wall elevations. Most kitchen components are represented here, including various types and sizes of drop-in and freestanding ranges, cooktops, grills, and refrigerators. Pay attention to details like door swings and drawer extensions (marked in dotted lines on these templates) as you consider the placement of these items in the room. If you don't see a template for something you'd like, draw your own.

Appliances

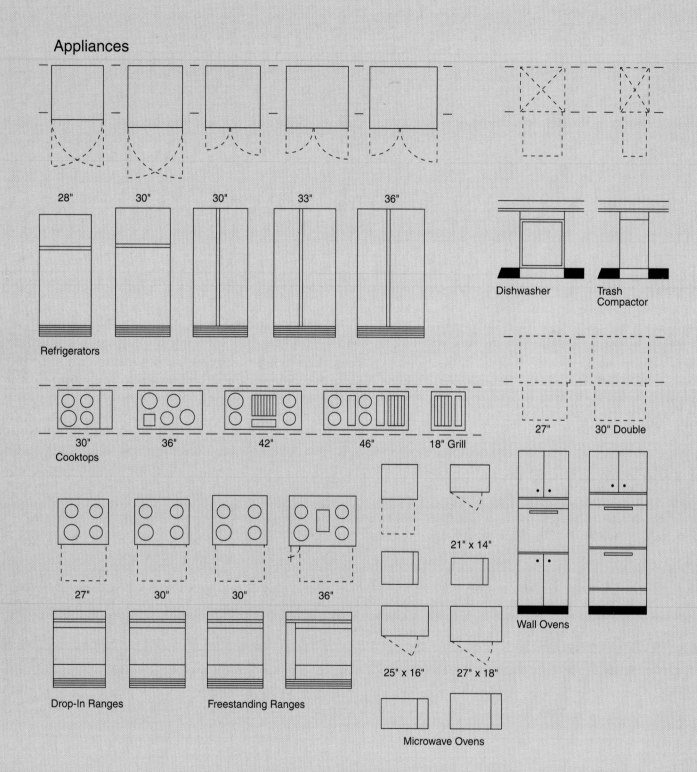

28"   30"   30"   33"   36"

Refrigerators

Dishwasher   Trash Compactor

30"   36"   42"   46"   18" Grill

Cooktops

27"   30" Double

Wall Ovens

27"   30"   30"   36"

21" x 14"

Drop-In Ranges   Freestanding Ranges

25" x 16"   27" x 18"

Microwave Ovens

Planning Grid

Use a photocopier to reproduce the grid at its original size, then cut out the templates on pages 278–280 to design your new or remodeled kitchen. Grid scale: 1 square equals 1 square foot.

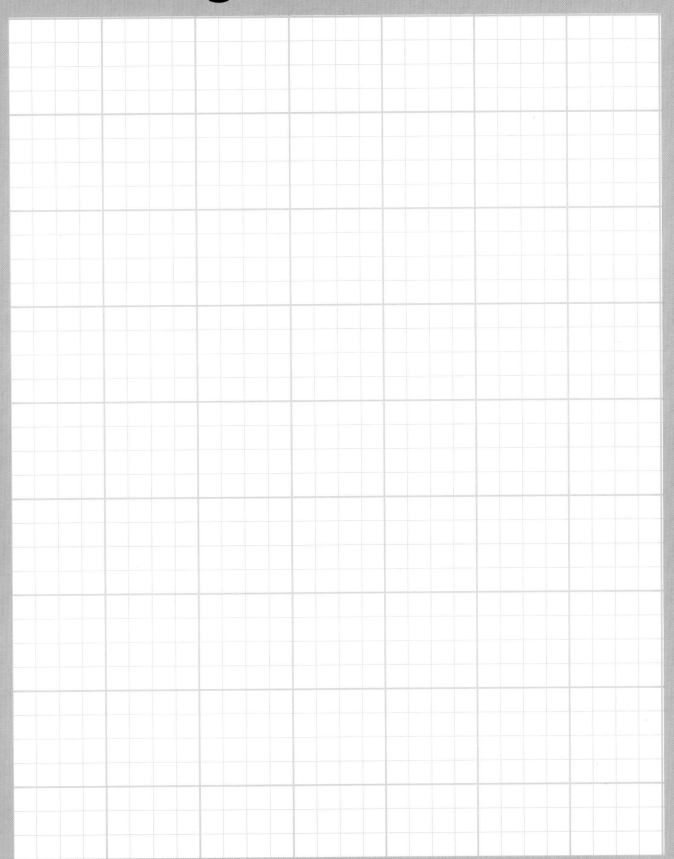

great american
kitchens
collection

designers

52

designers

Even More Inspiring Design!

■ If you enjoyed the dynamic decorating in this book, you'll love the beautiful kitchens in *Great American Kitchens*, Volume 1. It brings you sleek urban styles, Asian influences, bold jolts of color, and kitchens with country, French, and Tuscany accents. Start creating the kitchen of your dreams today—with *Great American Kitchens*, Volume 1.

ORDER TODAY—Call Sub-Zero at 1-800-222-7820 or visit www.subzero.com.

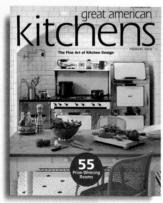

227

Lisa Masson Photography
511 Fourth Street
Annapolis, MD 21403
www.gmatsonphoto.com
Phone: 410-990-1777
Fax: 410-990-0057
lisa@lisamasson
 photography.com
www.lisamasson
 photography.com

G. Matson Photographic
3004 Forest Drive
Columbia, SC 29204
Phone/fax: 803-782-6597
woobieub@aol.com
www.gmatsonphoto.com

Kevin McGowan
5250 Gulfton #2G
Houston, TX 77081
Phone: 713-665-3818
kevin@kevinmcgowan.com
www.kevinmcgowan.com

Jeff McNamara Photography
In Focus Associates
305 East 46th Street
New York, NY 10017
Phone: 212-593-5100
Fax: 212-593-8087
ismeg@aol.com

Matthew Millman
 Photography
261 Bradford Street
San Francisco CA 94110
Phone: 415-577-3200
Fax: 415-401-6902
www.matthewmillman.com

Mike Moreland Photography
230 Broadmeadow Cove
Roswell, GA 30075
Phone: 770-993-6059
Fax: 770-998-7050
mmfoto@mindspring.com
www.morelandphoto.com

Keith Scott Morton
39 W. 29th Street, 11th Floor
New York, NY 10001
Phone: 212-889-6643
Fax: 212-683-3038
keith@ksmstudio.com
www.ksmstudio.com

Alise O'Brien
6995 Washington Avenue
St. Louis, MO 63130
Phone: 314-721-0285
Fax: 314-727-0125
aobphoto@sbcglobal.net
www.aliseobrienphotography.com

Jaime Pennel
320 N. 15th Street
Moorhead, MN 56560
Phone: 218-287-4221
farmhousestudio@
 yahoo.com

Gavin Peters
6505 E. Aberdeen
Wichita, KS 67206
Phone: 316-393-0454
Fax: 316-652-8778
gavin@gavinpeters.com
www.gavinpeters.com

Laurie Black Photography
172 Upper Lakeview Road
White Salmon, WA 98672
Phone: 509-493-8670
www.laurieblack.com

Fran Brennan Photography
2337 Tangley Road
Houston, TX 77005
Phone: 713-526-9206
mfranbrennan@aol.com

Chris Eden
Eden Arts
753 9th Avenue North
Seattle, WA 98109
Phone: 206-282-4788
Fax: 206-286-1639
edenarts@aa.net

Everett & Soulé
P.O. Box 150674
Altamonte Springs,
 FL 32715
Phone/fax: 407-831-4183
asoule@cfl.rr.com
www.portfolios.com/everettandsoule

Jeff Frey & Associates
405 E. Superior Street
Duluth, MN 55802
Phone: 218-722-6630
Fax: 218-722-8452
jfajeff@aol.com
www.freyphoto.com

Michael E. Garland
 Photography
3575 Colonial Avenue
Mar Vista, CA 90066
Phone: 310-572-7757
Fax: 310-572-0127
garland.photo@verizon.net

David Glomb
71340 Estellita Drive
Rancho Mirage, CA 92270
Phone: 760-340-4455
d.glomb@worldnet.att.net

Brian Griffin
Griffin Photodesign
3070 N.550 E.
Ogden, UT 84414
Phone: 801-782-7362
griffb@mac.com
www.griffinphotodesign.com

Hatch/Cloos Photography
P.O. Box 2274
Glenwood Springs, CO 81602
Phone: 970-945-6569
hatchphoto@sopris.net
www.mtnhomephoto.com

Tom Henry
Koechel, Peterson
 & Associates
2600 E. 26th Street
Minneapolis, MN 55406
Phone: 612-721-5017
Fax: 612-728-5559

Michael Hewes
429 Anacapa Street
Ventura, CA 93001
Phone: 805-643-0209
mikehewes@yahoo.com
www.michaelhewes.com

Nancy Hill Photography
677 N. Salem Road
Ridgefield, CT 06877
Phone/fax: 203-431-7655
nhill8006@sbcglobal.net

Christopher Hornsby
165 Bennett Avenue, #6M
New York, NY 10040
Phone: 212-942-3352
Fax: 212-569-3633
cthornsby@aol.com

Eduard Hueber
Archphoto Inc.
176 Grand Street,
 2nd Floor
New York, NY, 10013
Phone: 212-941-9294
Fax: 212-965-8830
archphotoinc@mac.com
www.archphoto.com

Jon Jensen Photography
2005 NE 50th Avenue
Portland, OR 97213
Phone: 503-493-9220
jjensenor@earthlink.net

Jenifer Jordan Photography
326 Blue Ribbon Road
Waxahachie, TX 75165
Phone: 972-845-2180
Fax: 214-845-2197
jjordanphoto@aol.com

Mike Kaskel Photography
5040 Warren, #407
Skokie, IL 60077
Phone: 847-675-8687
Fax: 847-675-8691
www.kaskelphoto.com

Curtis Laine
Studio23.US
23 Empire Drive
Saint Paul, MN 55103
Phone: 612-750-1526
Fax: 651-602-5601
studio23@eetc.com
www.studio23.us

Peter Leach
22 Denver Road
Denver, PA 17517
Phone: 717-336-7760
Fax: 717-336-6532
leachphoto@dejazzd.com

John Edward Linden
21820 De La Luz Ave.
Woodland Hills, CA 91364
Phone/fax: 818-888-8544
www.johnlinden
 photographs.com

To see more Great American Kitchens, contact your Sub-Zero/Wolf distributor.

■ For the name of a local dealer or to make an appointment at one of our wholesale distributors, call the closest office listed here. Many of these locations have operational kitchens where you can "test drive" the latest in cooking and refrigeration from Wolf and Sub-Zero. Their knowledgeable staff will review product options and refer you to a local dealer for the actual purchase.

index

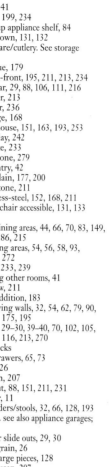